CHEROKEE
BOWS AND ARROWS

HOW TO MAKE AND SHOOT
PRIMITIVE BOWS AND ARROWS

AL HERRIN

al Herrin
1-8-93

FIRST EDITION

ᏆᏟ ᏃᎵᏔ White Bear Publishing, Tahlequah, Oklahoma

CHEROKEE BOWS AND ARROWS
How to Make and Shoot
Primitive Bows and Arrows

By Al Herrin

Published by:

White Bear Publishing
Dept. B
Rt.3 Box 172
Tahlequah, OK 74464 U.S.A.

Copyright © 1989 by Alan R. Herrin
    First Printing 1989

Printed in the United States of America

Publisher's Cataloging in Publication Data
Herrin, Alan R.
    Cherokee Bows and Arrows
    How to Make and Shoot
    Primitive Bows and Arrows.
    Bibliography:p.160
    Includes index.
1. Cherokee Indians--Arms and armor
2. Bows and Arrows.
I. Title
E99.C5H4 1989   739.73   89-051184
ISBN 0-9623601-3-9 Softcover

WHAT OTHERS ARE SAYING ABOUT THIS BOOK:

DR. JIM MILLER, KEARNEY STATE COLLEGE:
   "In today's high pressure, high tech world, this book is like a breath of fresh air. Many people are searching for a release from the ever increasing pressures of modern times and find that building and shooting primitive bows and arrows provides the release they need. Al Herrin takes the guess work out of the return to the primitive."
   "For archers and bowhunters: wait until you take your first trophy with your own self-made primitive bow! Try it, you'll like it!"

LINDA VANN, CHEROKEE HISTORICAL SOCIETY:
   "Dr. Herrin offers a remarkably informative, comprehensive, and one of a kind book. It is a much needed source that will fill a gap in the scarcity of literary materials related to the lifestyle of the Cherokee. Whether you are Indian or non-Indian and enjoy archery, hunting and nature, you will discover this book to be highly intriguing, educational and inspiring enough to make you want to attempt bow making."

MILES BEEN, OKLAHOMA BOWHUNTER:
   "I have been shooting and hunting with bow and arrow for about half of my 80 years of life, the last twenty years with a compound bow. A few months ago, I got a Cherokee bow from Al Herrin and I have been shooting it regularly since then. I haven't had so much fun with anything since I got a new red wagon for my fifth birthday! I can hardly wait for the hunting season to open."

ABOUT THE AUTHOR

Dr. Al Herrin is a member of the Cherokee Nation and was reared near Tahlequah, the capitol of the Cherokee Nation where he now lives with his wife, Frankie.

He began shooting the traditional Cherokee bows and arrows as a small child and made his first bow, which he still has, when he was eight years old. Over the years, his interest in bowmaking attracted the attention of several of the old Cherokee bowyers who taught him the secrets of their ancient craft.

Al is presently recognized by the Cherokee Historical Society as "an expert on the technical art of Cherokee archery", serves on the selection committee of the Cherokee Lost Arts Project, is a member of the intertribal "Native American Bowyers Association" and conducts workshops and seminars on Cherokee archery and bowmaking.

Al not only makes bows and arrows but uses them. He regularly competes in archery tournaments, including the Cherokee sport of cornstalk shooting, and hunts small and large game with his bows and arrows. He has written extensively for newspapers and magazines on the topics of Cherokee culture and bowhunting.

Dr. Herrin possesses a unique combination of cultural background, instruction by traditional bowyers, and natural abilities in woodworking, archery and writing that is possesed by no other living person. The result is this book which will become a classic.

ACKNOWLEDGMENTS

Several people helped in the preparation of this book; with technical assistance, proofreading, photography, good advice, etc. They are Miles Been, Jerry Day, Elray DeRoin, Col. Martin Hagerstrand, Melissa Herrin, Wayne Kindell, Dr. Jim Miller, Rev. Charlie Morris, Jane Phillips, Dr. Gerri Porter, Linda Vann, and David Wren.

I make special acknowledgment and dedicate this book, with love, to my wife, FRANKIE PARRIS HERRIN. She gave me the time to hunt and fish and write this book.

Al Herrin, Ph.D.
Tahlequah, Oklahoma
July, 1989

Cover by Jeanine Pamplin.

TABLE OF CONTENTS

WARNING--DISCLAIMER

This book is designed to provide information in regard to the subject matter covered. Every effort has been made to make this book as acccurate and complete as possible. However, much of the information contained in this book has previously been passed through the generations of Cherokees orally and, as such, there is the possibility of different methods of doing things, errors and omissions. There may be mistakes both typographical and in content. Therefore, the reader should use common sense and his or her own experience along with the guidance of this book in using tools, gathering materials, making bows, arrows and bowstrings and in the use of the bows and arrows.

The purpose of this book is to educate and entertain. The author and White Bear Publishing shall have neither liability nor responsibility to any person or entity for any injury, loss or damage caused or alleged to be caused directly or indirectly by the information contained in this book.

CHAPTER 1

WHY MAKE OR SHOOT A PRIMITIVE BOW?

Most modern archers refer to the bows used by the American Indians before the coming of the white man as "primitive" bows. I will use that term in this book but the reader should understand that the term "primitive" does not imply that those bows were not efficient weapons. In the hands of Indian hunters and warriors, they were highly efficient and deadly weapons.

In the Cherokee culture of today, as among all modern American Indian tribes, the making and shooting of traditional, primitive bows and arrows are rapidly becoming lost arts. Most of the old bowyers (bow-makers) are gone and few of the younger generation seem willing to learn the knowledge, patience and skill needed to make or shoot the traditional bows and arrows.

To most archers today, including Cherokees, it seems easier and makes more sense to buy a mass produced compound bow and aluminum arrows which will shoot faster and more accurately than any primitive bow. The traditional instinctive shooting style is also fading; being replaced by more precise methods using sights and mechanical releases.

The question arises as to why anyone would want to make or shoot a primitive bow when they could have a modern coumpound bow. After all, isn't accuracy the goal of every archer and the responsibility of every bowhunter? Of course, but shooting accurately and killing game are not the only goals of importance; if they were, then the next logical question would be "Why shoot a compound bow when you could have a rifle"? It would be like asking a jogger, "Why jog when you could ride in a car?" It would be a fair question if getting to a destination were the only goal.

A goal of archers and bowhunters is to become as accurate as they can become within the limits of their chosen equipment, style of shooting and physical capabilities. They choose their equipment based upon practical considerations such as what they can afford, their physical limitations, what their friends are using, and the kind of shooting they plan to do. They may also be influenced in choice of equipment by less practical, intangible considerations such as the history and romance of archery and hunting and the desire to preserve the Indian culture.

Perhaps more important than all these other feelings, as a reason for choosing certain equipment, is the love of a challenge. This is especially true for bowhunters. Under the limitations of their equipment and the laws regulating bowhunting, modern bowhunters confront the challenge of a fair and equal contest between their hunting skill and equipment and the keen senses and instincts of the wild creatures they hunt. A true bowhunter can derive more satisfaction from a good stalk or a well placed tree stand resulting in a close-range shot, even if the shot is missed, than from a long-range kill with a rifle.

Therefore, we might say that the goal of the modern sport of bowhunting is to kill game but under self-imposed constraints that make it a fair and equal contest between the hunter and the animal. Bowhunters even the contest by putting constraints upon the equipment they use; choosing the bow and arrow because they feel that the rifle shifts the balance in the contest too much in favor of the hunter. Some bowhunters choose the English longbow or the traditional Indian bow over the compound bow for the same reason, to increase the challenge.

As the hunters' equipment becomes more primitive, they must compensate by improving their hunting abilities if the contest is not to shift too much in the favor of the animals they hunt. The early Indians used the most primitive of equipment and shooting methods with good success because of supurb hunting skill which enabled them to get close shots.

For this writer, the ultimate challenge and therefore the ultimate satisfaction in bowhunting is to emulate the hunting of the early Indians; including making a good, dependable bow and arrows from materials found in nature, learning to shoot them with reasonable accuracy, and developing enough hunting skill to consistantly take game with them. This writer hopes that others will try this ultimate challenge and help to preserve the art of making, shooting and hunting with primitive bows and arrows.

Photo by Elray DeRoin.

CHAPTER 2

MY CHEROKEE HERITAGE

Even as a small boy, I wondered about my ability to survive if a nuclear war or some other catastrophe should destroy our civilization and I was forced to get food, shelter, etc. from nature. These thoughts did not bring fear but rather the feelings of adventure. Although I lived in twentieth century civilization, I felt I should be living in an earlier time, roaming the vast, unfenced plains and mountains with bow and arrows in hand as my Cherokee ancestors had done; depending upon my knowledge of nature and my skills as a hunter to survive.

For me, the love of bows, arrows and hunting was a cultural inheritance as well as a natural outgrowth of my love of nature and my fascination with survival. My cultural inheritance came from both my

Cherokee and my English ancestors. My father was an original enrollee of the Oklahoma Cherokees. My mother was of English blood and decended from generations of mountain folk who had hunted and trapped in the Appalachians, Smokies and Ozarks. I was reared near Tahlequah, Oklahoma, the capitol of the Cherokee Nation where my wife, Frankie, and I now live. Frankie is the granddaughter, several times removed, of the famous Cherokee Chief, John Ross.

Richard McLemore, a Cherokee who was like a second father to me, lived up McLemore Hollow, a couple of miles from my boyhood home in the Cherokee Nation. Richard made my first bow and arrows for me when I was a small child. The little bow was carved from osage orange wood and was about three feet long. It had a string made of rawhide from a fox squirrel. It was of the typical Cherokee design, without any sign of a handle, so that it bent in one smooth arc the entire length of the bow, like the letter D.

The arrows were made from dogwood sprouts sized and smoothed with a pocket knife and pieces of broken glass. The feathers were from a red-tailed hawk and tied to the shaft with sinew. The nocks, grooves in the back end of the arrows for taking the bowstring, were shallow notches carved in the wood so that, rather than sliding around the bowstring, the nock was held against the string with the thumb and forefinger. The arrows had no metal points but were left blunt and blackened in a fire to harden the wood. I wanted metal "barrel hoop" points like Richard made for his small game arrows, but Richard said my mother might not let me use the arrows if they looked too

14

dangerous.

I practiced mostly by shooting into a bale of hay; The abundant flint rocks of the Cherokee hills prohibited the shooting of precious arrows carelessly. Occasionally, I had the special treat of a cardboard box my father would bring home from Tahlequah. The arrows made a satisfying "whack" when they went through the box and I would shoot the box until it fell into pieces.

I soon became a deadly shot at close range and began hunting with the bow, regularly taking rabbits, rats, birds and ocassional squirrels from the surrounding woods and fields and frogs, fish and snakes from Barron Fork Creek. I even killed a few of my mother's guineas that drove me crazy with their infernal calling while I was doing my chores around the barn and a couple of roosters that loved to crow just outside my window at the crack of dawn. When my mother missed the guineas and chickens and mentioned it, I said "Probably a fox is getting them." To which my father gave me a knowing look and replied, "Well, if I catch that fox getting them, I'll tan his hide so he can't sit down for a week!" The fox didn't kill any more poultry after that.

Nuclear war never came, thank God, but I still enjoyed "playing" at survival and dreaming of days of long ago. I roamed the forest and streams with my father, with Richard and others and learned the skills of the hunter. I listened to the Cherokee elders tell glorious stories of hunting and war and I learned to make and shoot the traditional Cherokee bows and arrows.

But, like all boys, I thought I wanted something better than the homemade bows I

was shooting and, when I was in high
school, I finally got a second-hand Bear
Kodiak recurved bow laminated with
fiberglass. I became active in
competitive archery and, over the years, I
went to progressively "better" archery
equipment and more gadgets, trying to keep
up with each advance in archery
technology. Although I still enjoyed
shooting and hunting, I had the nagging
feeling that it just wasn't as good as it
used to be.

Finally, with the invention of the
compound bow, something inside me snapped
and said, "Enough!" Things had gotten too
far away from what archery should be. I
discarded my gadgets, returned to my
primitive bows and arrows and rediscovered
the romance of archery which I had thought
was gone forever.

A few of my Cherokee relations and
friends were not enthusiastic about my
writing this book. I reveal secrets that,
in the old days, were passed down from
bowyer to apprentice and were known to few
others. Unfortunately, the old system has
broken down in modern times. Most of the
old bowyers have gone without passing
their secrets to others so that the art of
making traditional bows and arrows is
almost lost. Unless a different method of
passing the information is used, the art
will be lost. I decided to write this
book to help preserve the knowledge of
primitive archery and to encourage others
to rediscover this important part of our
Indian and American culture. I have often
felt discouraged because the preservation
of our cultural heritage seems important
to so few. But perhaps that is enough for
now and someday others will understand.

I watch the eagles catching fish in

16

the Illinois River that flows by my house,
watch the beavers swim by and the deer
come to the river to drink. When I was a
child in this place, there were no eagles,
beavers or deer. They had been
exterminated by the march of civilization
and technology. But they were brought
back by a few people who realized the
importance of preserving these things from
our past before they were lost forever.

Our technological progress has made us
what we are but our roots in the past make
us who we are. If we do not know who we
are and take pride in our heritage, then
we will not only lose our arts, we will
surely lose ourselves.

Photo by Elray DeRoin.

CHAPTER 3

THE PRIMITIVE BOW

Modern American archers have inherited a rich tradition of archery from the archers of England and other parts of the old world and from the Cherokees and other Indian archers that were native to the New World. It has been said that England was built on a base of iron arrowheads. During the 14th and 15th centuries, the English archers with their longbows were legendary in warfare. In even earlier times, the legendary Cherokee archers with their longbows established dominance over an area of eastern North America that was almost as large as England.

But the beginnings of archery occurred long before either the Cherokees or English were nations and we can only guess when and where the first bow and arrows were made. The best estimates place the

19

invention of the bow and arrow about 12,000 years ago. Although we are uncertain about the beginning, we can be certain of the impact of the bow and arrow on history. In virtually every area of the world, except what is now Australia, the bow and arrow was a major factor in the fates of men and nations.

The first bow was probably a springy stick of wood with a string of some type tied on it and the arrow was a smaller, straight piece of wood. During the twelve thousand years from that time to the twentieth century the bow and arrow remained basically unchanged. Typically, it was a wood "self" bow, meaning it derived its power entirely from the wood it was made from.

A few isolated modifications occurred, such as recurved bow tips, backings of sinew, and bows made of materials such as horn or bone. These modifications were usually adopted because good bow wood was not available in some areas or extremely short bows were needed to shoot from horseback. Substitute materials, such as horn and sinew were used to prevent the breaking of inferior woods or extremely short bows. However, the vast majority of primitive bows were self bows made entirely of wood.

Scientists generally agree that the ancestors of the American Indians migrated across the Bering Strait from Asia. During the Ice Ages, a large amount of the earth's water became frozen in glaciers so that the level of the ocean was lowered and a land bridge was exposed across the Bering Strait. Perhaps twenty thousand years ago, before the invention of the bow and arrow, early hunters, pursuing Ice Age mammals such as the wooly mammoth, crossed the land bridge, migrated down through western Canada, spread through north and central America and finally to the tip of South America. The migration was in not one but many waves over many thousands of years. As the groups became isolated from one another for long periods of time, the languages and customs changed until they became the hundreds of different Indian tribes living in the Americas when Columbus arrived.

The bow and arrow was probably brought to the Americas by the migrating hunters. Evidence indicates that the earliest of the migrating hunters did not have the bow and arrow but used a dart or short spear thrown by a hand-held stick called an atlatl. The bow and arrow appeared later, probably brought by a later wave of hunters after its invention somewhere in Asia, Europe or Africa. A cane arrow shaft of Cherokee design was unearthed in Tennessee in 1956 and dated as being over 2000 years old. When first contacted by white explorers in 1540, the Chrokees were still using arrows made from that same type of cane.

The bows and arrows and shooting ability of the American Indians have, by some, been criticized as being of poor quality compared to other cultures and other times. The only point of importance, however, is that the American Indian was a hunter and warrior first and an archer second. His equipment and shooting abilities were adequate for his requirements in hunting and warfare and making comparisons between his skills and those of the modern archer are pointless.

Reports of early explorers in what is now the southeastern United States leave little doubt that the Indian archers and their equipment were effective. A chronicler of the De Soto expedition in 1540 wrote:

They never remain quiet, but are continually running, traversing from place to place, so that neither crossbow or arquebuse can be aimed at them. Before a Christian can make a single shot with either, an Indian will discharge three or four arrows: and he seldom misses of his object. Where the arrow meets with no armour, it pierces as deeply as the shaft from a crossbow. Their bows are very perfect; the arrows are made of certain canes, like reeds, very heavy, and so stiff that one of them, when sharpened, will pass through a target. Some are pointed with a bone of a fish, sharp like a chisel; others with some stone like a point of diamond; of such the great number, when they strike upon armour, break at the place the parts are put together; those of cane will split, and will enter a shirt of mail, doing more injury than when armed.

In one of many battles with the Indians, 22 of De Soto's Spaniards were killed and 148 others were wounded. There were a total of 688 arrow wounds. Seven horses were killed, three shot completely through both shoulders, and twenty-nine wounded.

According to a chronicler's account, "The arrow shots were tremendous, and sent with such a will and force that the lance of one gentleman named Nuno de Tovar, made of two pieces of ash and very good, was pierced by an arrow in the middle, as by an auger, without being split, and the arrow made a cross with the lance."

I have personally shot enough game with Cherokee bows to offer a qualified opinion on their effectiveness. I usually hunt big game with a bow pulling about 60 to 80 pounds and draw an 11/32 inch diameter wood arrow 28 inches. A hit in the chest cavity of a big game animal such as deer, elk, or bear almost always results in complete penetration, often cutting through ribs on each side and, often, the arrow flies completely through and sticks in the ground beyond. I have no doubt that the descriptions of the early explorers, quoted above, are accurate.

During the past 50 years, great changes have occured in archery equipment; first with the invention of fiberglass and then the invention of the compound bow. For 12,000 years the bow and arrow had remained the same, made entirely from materials found in nature. Suddenly, the basic concept of the bow changed and bows and arrows were made entirely from man-made synthetic materials. A modern compound bow with all the modern gadgets shooting aluminum arrows with plastic vanes would probably not be recognizable as a bow and arrow by the archers of old.

An increasing number of archers share my feeling that modern archery has lost something vital in the stampede to gadgetry. They are turning away from the gadgets and rediscovering what J. Maurice Thompson called "the Witchery of Archery" with a 12,000 year tradition of simplicity; a springy stick with a string and a straight stick for an arrow!

In this book, I attempt to present a practical approach to making and shooting primitive bows and arrows. This means I strive to maintain the spirit of primitive archery but not to the total exclusion of modern technology. For example, I will suggest that you make your bow using steel hand tools rather than tools of flint and bone as the old Indians used. I will introduce you to the concept of accurately measuring arrow spine or stiffness, which was unknown to the ancient arrowmaker, because it allows you to make better arrows. I have freely used knowledge which comes from bowyers and arrowmakers of the English tradition as well as from American Indian cultures other than my own Cherokee culture. My main purpose is to present enough information for you to choose your own path to the enjoyment of primitive archery.

CHAPTER 4

BOW WOODS

Almost any wood and some other natural materials such as horn and antler can be used to make a bow but some are better than others, depending on how "springy" the material is. For example, bows that are identical in design and draw weight but made from different woods will vary greatly in "cast" or how much force is imparted to the arrow. The wood or other material making up the bow is bent when the bow is drawn and the cast is related to (1)the amount of force required to bend the bow and (2) the "springiness" or ability of the material in the bow to quickly straighten out when the string is released.

Bowyers generally agree that the best wood for self bows is osage orange (Maclura pomifera) and it is the wood I will use in this book to illustrate making bows. Osage Orange is also known as Bois d'Arc (pronounced bow-darc), hedge apple, mock orange and other names. In the Cherokee language, we call it Galogwekdi Dalonige which means yellow locust. Although it makes a good bow, it is difficult wood to work. A good osage orange bow stave is like a good wife; it is hard to find and can be, all at the same time, the most stubborn, frustrating, humbling, and satisfying thing a man ever tangled with.

Compared to other bow woods, osage orange has excellent cast, is tough and can take rough treatment, and is little affected by extremes of temperature or moisture. One problem with osage orange is that most of the trees are not suitable for bows. Based upon my own experience in hunting and cutting osage orange for bows, I estimate that only one to two percent of the trees will yield suitable wood. The other 98 to 99 percent are too crooked, twisted or have too many small limbs to be used. Another problem with osage orange is that, even after you have found a good bow stave, the wood is difficult to work.

In prehistoric times, an extensive network of trade routes existed through the southern and eastern part of what is now the United States over which osage orange bow wood was traded. The source of most of the best wood was the basin of the Red River between the present states of Oklahoma and Texas and the basin of the Arkansas River through Arkansas, Oklahoma and into Kansas. The logs were split-out and dressed-down where the trees were cut and then the wood transported by water and overland trails for hundreds of miles to the traditional territory of the Cherokees and other tribes. The Cherokees and other tribes traded for the wood which they then worked down to finished bows.

Today, osage orange is much more widely available than it was in pre-Columbian times. Beginning in the 1930's, osage orange was planted extensively as windbreaks around fields so that now the tree is found over much of the United States. The tree has spread from original plantings to become a nuisance in some places. Since the tree has little economic value except for fence posts, and wooden posts have largely been replaced by steel posts in recent times, it is often possible to get permission from a landowner to cut a tree or limb to make a bow.

Other woods, such as black locust, white mulberry, sassafras, red hickory, ironwood, white ash, white oak, red cedar, and elm can be used to make self bows. Yew, a soft wood of the Taxaceae family, which grows on the Pacific Coast, is good bow wood but it is more sensitive to temperature extremes and not as rugged as osage orange. Yew grows in England and was considered the best wood for making the famous English longbows of olden times, but they didn't have osage orange and I suspect, if they had, they would have considered yew as second best. I have some bows of lemonwood, a wood from Cuba and South America, that was popular for making bows in the twentieth century United States before the invention of fiberglass. Some archers of that period, such as Howard Hill, used laminated bamboo bows, which shot beautifully but probably should not be classified as "self" bows.

The ancient Cherokees, in their homeland in the southeast, had access to several good bow woods but preferred black locust for bows. This is still the favored local wood used by Eastern Cherokee bowyers on the Qualla Reservation in North Carolina. When the main body of the Cherokees were forcibly removed to Oklahoma, bowyers found an abundance of osage orange. It is the wood of choice for Western Cherokee bowyers today, although black locust, hickory, and other bow woods grow in the area.

FIGURE 4-1: Staves of Bow Wood on the Author's Shop Porch.

CHAPTER 5

OSAGE ORANGE

The osage orange tree got its name from the Osage Indians who inhabited part of the pre-Columbian range of the tree and from its fruit which resembles a large, rough green orange in shape and surface texture. The early French explorers named the tree Bois d'Arc which translates in English to "wood of the bow" because they found it was highly prized by the Indians for making bows.

Mature trees are usually twenty to forty feet in height and four to twelve inches in diameter although trees sixty feet tall and three feet in diameter are found. The branches are quite thorny amd the bark is thin, gray and sometimes tinged with yellow or orange. The sexes are seperated with male flowers on one tree and female on another. Only the female tree bears fruit.

When cut, the wood emits a thick, sticky, milky sap. The sapwood, immediately beneath the bark, is whitish to yellowish in color. The heartwood is bright yellow to orange in color and darkens to a deep brown upon long exposure. I have seen Cherokee bows, over a hundred yeas old, that were such a dark brown they were almost black. However, the Cherokee practice of rubbing bear oil or hog lard on the bow adds to the darkening of the wood.

Osage orange wood is very heavy with few woods in the world having a higher density, in fact, it will barely float in water. It is also very durable when exposed to conditions in which other woods would soon rot. For this reason, it was used for fence posts and it was not unusual for an untreated osage orange corner post to last for 50 to 100 years. The yellow wood contains a dye that has been extracted commercially and used to dye khaki military uniforms.

Leaf and Fruit, one-quarter natural size.   Twig, two-thirds natural size.

FIGURE 5-1: Osage Orange (From Forest Trees of Oklahoma).

CHAPTER 6

TOOLS

You can make a bow with a few simple hand tools (Figure 6-1). After all, the old Indians made them with tools of stone, bone and wood! Besides an axe or saw to cut the log and a sledge and some steel wedges to split the log, you will need a draw-knife, a wood rasp, a vise or shaving horse, a scraper (broken glass will do), and some sandpaper. I avoid using power tools such as band saws, jointers, sanders, etc. They are designed to speed-up the process and therein lies their problem. Most of your mistakes will come from getting in a hurry and, by using hand tools, you will make fewer mistakes. Buy tools of good quality and keep them sharp. You can probably find an old draw knife at a garage sale, flea market or junk store. The old tools often have

31

better steel than new ones. Buy a good quality wood rasp from a hardware store. Mine is a Nicholson rasp about ten inches long, flat on one side and rounded on the other, with a course and fine set of teeth on each side. With the rasp, you can remove wood without "digging in" which often happens when using a draw knife or other cutting tool on osage orange.

You might want to make a shaving horse; they are easy to make and work better than a vice for holding your bow. Mine, which is shown in Figure 6-2, has a main beam (6'X6"X2"), two short legs (11"X1-1/2"X3/4"),two long legs (2'X1-1/2"X3/4"), one arm (26"X1-1/2"X2"), one block (5"X3-1/2"X3"), and a foot pedal (16"X3-3/4"X3/4").

I have a shop but I prefer to work on bows out-of-doors. I set my shaving horse and other tools under a shade tree near my wood pile which is about 30 yards from the bank of the river. I rough out the stave with an axe and chopblock and use the shaving horse to hold the stave while I use the draw knife or rasp. If the stave is crooked or twisted, I build a little fire to heat it and then use the forked limbs of the shade tree for bending the stave until it is straight. I can do anything I could do in a million dollar shop and also feel the breeze and hear the birds--and I don't have to sweep up the shavings!

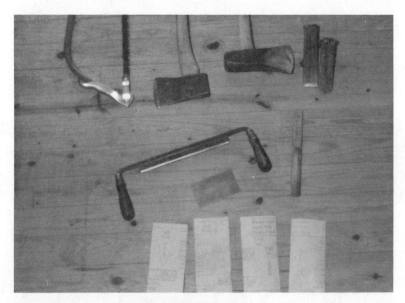

FIGURE 6-1: Bowmaking Tools.

FIGURE 6-2: Shaving Horse

Cartoon by David Wren.

CHAPTER 7

TIME AND YOUR MIND

The biggest enemy to your success in making a bow is your own mind. You are the product of our modern society with its emphasis on time and getting things done quickly. If you get in a hurry while making your bow, you will probably ruin it.

The traditional Cherokees had a concept of time that was very different from most people today. The story is told about a Cherokee farmer who was visited by an efficiency expert. The expert watched as the farmer let a hog out of the pen, drove it down to the creek to drink, and then drove it back to the pen. Then the farmer repeated the process with a second hog and so on until all twenty hogs in the pen had been watered. The efficiency expert pointed out to the farmer that a great deal of time could be saved by driving all twenty hogs to the water at the same time. The old farmer scratched his head, thought a minute and replied, "I guess it would be all right but, really, time ain't all that important to a hog."

People often ask how long it takes me to make a primitive longbow. I truthfully answer, "I don't know--as long as it takes, I guess." Each tree, each stave, each person is different so that it is impossible to place a completion time on the task of making a bow. The old Cherokee bowmakers who taught me would say "What difference does it make? If you are doing something you like, then why hurry? If you don't like it, then why are you doing it?"

But if you insist on putting it in a time frame, I probably spend an average of about five hours per stave in locating, cutting, transporting, splitting, removing the bark, and dipping the ends of the stave. Then, the stave is seasoned for two to five years before I use it for bows. Then, from that stage to a completed bow takes about forty to fifty hours of work. Some have told me I could make my bows faster but I am interested in making them good, not fast. Unlike the hog, time is important to a bow.

CHAPTER 8

TYPES OF BOWS

Perhaps we should begin with a
comparison of the Cherokee longbow with
the English longbow. This book is about
Cherokee bows and arrows but both the
Cherokee longbow and the English longbow
are simple, self bows and there are enough
similarities between them to justify a
comparison. Also, there exists a written
record of the making and use of English
longbows in 1545 in the book, Toxophilus
which, coincidentally, was only five years
after the Spanish explorer DeSoto made the
first contact, by a European, with the
Cherokees and described their bows and
arrows. Our goal is learning so I will
freely refer to any source of useful
knowledge about longbows.
    Although there are similarities
between the Cherokee longbow and the

English longbow, there are significant
differences you should consider in
choosing a design for your bow. The
primary difference is in the
cross-sectional shape of the limbs (Figure
8-1). The Cherokee bow has limbs that
are, in cross section, considerably wider
than they are thick. The limbs are flat
on the "back", the side that is away from
you as you shoot the bow, and either flat
or slightly rounded on the "belly", the
side that is toward you when you shoot the
bow. The English longbow has limbs that
are, in cross section, narrower and
thicker than the Cherokee bow. The limbs
are flat on the back and greatly rounded,
like a letter U, on the belly. I have
tried both designs and I am convinced that
the Cherokee design is better.

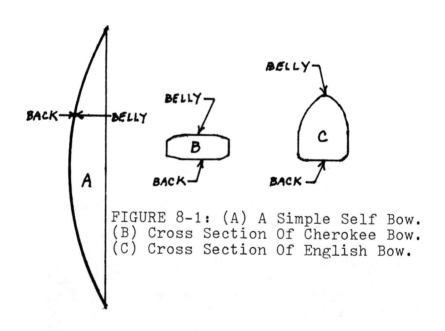

FIGURE 8-1: (A) A Simple Self Bow.
(B) Cross Section Of Cherokee Bow.
(C) Cross Section Of English Bow.

When a bow is drawn, the wood on the back is subjected to tension and the wood on the belly is subjected to compression. The U shaped belly on the English longbow concentrates the compression in a thin line down the center of the belly which greatly increases the stress on the wood whereas the flat belly of the Cherokee bow distributes the compression over the entire wide surface of the belly. I have had several osage orange bows, made on the design of the English longbow, literally explode while I was shooting them because of this stress on the belly. I have never had a similar experience with an osage orange bow of Cherokee design.

Another advantage of the Cherokee over the English design is in the amount of "string follow" in the bows (Figure 8-2). String follow is an undesirable condition and refers to the bow retaining some bend even after the string is removed. Bows that I have made on the English design

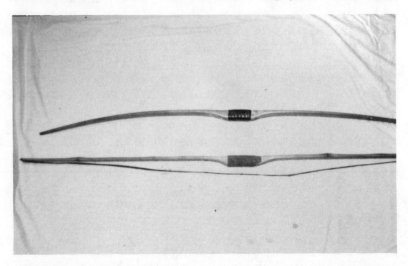

FIGURE 8-2: String Follow. Upper bow shows string follow; lower bow shows none.

from both osage orange and American yew tend to follow the string, although the yew wood shows more string follow than does the osage orange. This is due to the breakdown of the wood cells in the belly because of too much stress. My bows made of osage orange on the Cherokee design show little if any string follow. So, I would advise you to pattern your bow after the Cherokee rather than the English design.

Cherokee bows can be categorized into two types based upon whether or not there is a handle section (Figure 8-3). For this discussion, we will refer to those without a handle section as "D" bows since they bend in a smooth arc over their entire length and look like a letter D when strung. Those with a handle section we will call "handle" bows. There is considerable variation in the handle, with some bows having the limbs only slightly narrowed at .the handle and the handle only slightly thicker than the average thickness of the limbs. Other handles are narrowed considerably from the average width of the limbs and, in thickness, are raised well above the line of the belly of the bow. But regardless of variations, the handle bow has a non-bending middle section while the D bow bends over its entire length. Both types have advantages and disadvantages so you need to determine which type is best for you before beginning to work on your bow.

Most of the traditional bows among the Cherokees in Eastern Oklahoma are "D" bows, rectangular in cross section and are five to six feet in length. These bows usually have their maximum width of about 1 1/2 inches in the center, where the handle would be on a handle bow, and are

FIGURE 8-3: Cherokee Bows. The D bow is on
the left, the handle bow on the right.

between 1 inch and 1 1/4 inch wide at the tips. The nocks are large and cut like a "V" so that the tips are diamond shaped. The edges of the large nocks are left unsmoothed to assist in holding the traditional rawhide string. Since there is no arrow rest, the shooter uses his first finger or knuckle for a rest.

One advantage of the D bow is that it is relatively easy to make, since there is no handle section, and tillering (getting the limbs to bend evenly and equally) is not difficult. Another advantage is long life. Because the whole bow bends, there is less stress on the limbs than in a handle bow of the same length so these bows will last a long time. Also, if we compare a D bow and a handle bow of the same length, the D bow can take a longer arrow or, put another way, you can use a shorter D bow to shoot the same arrow. For example, a five foot D bow can take a 28 inch draw but, a handle bow of almost six foot is needed for a 28 inch draw.

The biggest disadvantage of the D bow, in my opinion, is that it is unpleasant to shoot. Since there is no handle section, you must hold the flat, edged middle of the bow which is not comfortable and also you always wonder if you are gripping it in the same place each time. Because of the design, these bows tend to kick in your hand when you shoot them. Also, because of the width of the center, the arrow sticks out to the left (for a right handed shooter) when nocked and seems that it would tend to shoot far to the left but actually the effect is small. The arrow quickly straightens its flight and you learn to compensate for any tendency to shoot to the left.

The handle bows are the type I prefer,

mainly because they are "sweeter" shooting and kick less than the D bows. Another advantage to the handle bow is that you have an arrow rest so your arrow is in the same place with each shot. Of course, there is nothing to prevent your putting an arrow rest on a D bow. Another advantage to the handle bow is that the handle section is thinner than the bow limbs so that the arrow is nearer the center line of the bow. Finally, you can use "billets", half the length of a stave, to build a handle bow. The depth and thickness of the non-bending handle section allows you to make a strong splice joint to join the billets.

The disadvantages of the handle bows are that they are more difficult to make and tiller properly and must be longer than the D bow to handle the same arrow.

Before we leave our discussion of bow types, I will mention that there are other types of bows which we will not discuss in detail because they are not within the scope of this book on Cherokee bows and arrows and they have no features that would help you to make a better bow. These other types are generally very short or very long bows which were used by some tribes.

The short "horse bows" usually had a backing of sinew, recurved tips, and reflexed limbs. The little bows were designed for a specific purpose; close range shots from horseback at buffalo. They were still in use by the plains Indians when Catlin and other artists painted them in the 1800's. Those paintings gained widespread fame and, as a result, the horse bows are what many people think of as "Indian" bows. Actually, only a handful of the hundreds of tribes in North and South America used such bows. To my knowledge, the Cherokees never used bows of that type. The Cherokee longbow was superior to the horse bow in accuracy, effective range, penetrating power and durability in wet weather. Although the Cherokees knew how to put sinew backing on a bow, there was no need for it on a longbow made of good bow wood.

Likewise, the grotesquely long bows and arrows used by some South American Indians represent another type which I will not discuss in detail because, once again, the Cherokees did not use them and they have no features that are superior to those of the Cherokee bow.

CHAPTER 9

BOWS AND ARROWS; LENGTH AND SPINE

One of the first decisions you should make before beginning to work on your bow, is to decide on the length you want your bow to be. The length refers to the distance between the bow nocks, not from tip to tip. The proper length depends on several factors such as what you plan to use the bow for, your height, and the length of arrows you plan to shoot. If you plan to shoot at buffalo from the back of a running horse, you might want a very short bow of three or four feet in length. But for most other uses, a longer bow of five to six feet in length is better.

Probably the best way to decide on a bow length is to first consider your physical stature, use that to determine the arrow length you should shoot and then determine the length of bow you need to shoot arrows of that length. One important thing to remember is that it is an advantage to shoot as short an arrow as you can comfortably handle, which is exactly opposite to what many modern archers think. A primitive bow is shot differently from a compound bow so most archers use a shorter draw length with a primitive bow than they would use with a compound. Of course, you should also remember that aluminum arrows are recommended for compound bows while, in this book, we are referring only to arrows made of wood or other natural materials.

Your "draw length" is the distance from the bowstring to the back of the bow handle, where your arrow would be, at your full draw (Figure 9-1). Your overall arrow length, including nock and head, will be two to four inches longer than your draw length, depending on the length of your nock, arrowhead and some other factors we will discuss in Chapter 22. But, for now, we are concerned with your draw length rather than the overall length of your arrows. Your draw length depends mostly on the length of your arms, which is related to your height, and your "anchor point", which is the place you draw the arrow to each time you shoot. For example, my anchor point is the middle finger of my right hand at the corner of my mouth which is where I draw my arrow and "anchor" or hold before I release (Figure 9-2).

A good way to determine the draw length that is right for you is to put a yardstick against the center of your breastbone and hold it between your two hands stretched straight out in front of your body (Figure 9-3). Where your middle fingers reach will give you your

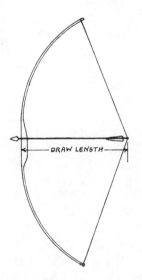

FIGURE 9-1: DRAW LENGTH

FIGURE 9-2:
Anchor Point.

FIGURE 9-3:
Yardstick Test.

approximate draw length. I am six feet three inches tall and the "yardstick test" shows my draw length should be 28-1/2 inches. I shortened it a half inch without any difficulty and use a draw length of 28 inches. A longbow is shot with the bow arm slightly bent at the elbow and that makes the 28 inch draw comfortable for me. If you are less than six feet tall, you can comfortably use a draw length of 27 inches or shorter.

There is a definite advantage to shooting arrows of a 28 inch or shorter draw length in primitive longbows. Basically, by shooting a shorter arrow, you can use a smaller diameter shaft and still get the stiffness you need in the arrow. To shoot properly, wooden arrows must have the correct "spine" or stiffness to match the weight of your bow; the heavier the bow, the stiffer the arrow must be to shoot properly. The spine is dependent on the length, diameter and consistency of the wood in the arrow shaft. The longer the draw length of the arrow, the larger the diameter must be in order for the shaft to have sufficient spine. We will discuss more about arrow size and spine in Chapter 24.

Now that you have determined the draw length you should shoot, how do you determine the length of the bow needed to shoot those arrows? A rule-of-thumb which came from the old English bowyers was that a bow six feet long would shoot an arrow with a draw length of 28 inches. The Cherokees also handed down a tradition regarding length of bows and arrows. Many Cherokee D bows are about five to five and one half feet long and are used with arrows 28 inches long. The Cherokee bow could be made shorter than the English bow because the Cherokee bow had a better cross-sectional design and was made from a better bow wood, as we discussed in Chapter 8.

T.M. Hamilton, in his book <u>Native American Bows</u>, states that, for maximum efficiency in self bows, the "ideal" ratio of bow length to arrow length is two to one; that is, the bow should be twice the length of the arrow. He also says that at this ratio, the bow is on the verge of breaking because it is so highly stressed. I'm not sure how he arrived at this two to one ratio because he quotes no authority and I have never seen the figure used elsewhere. But even if that is the ratio at which a self bow is working at maximum efficiency, if the bow is on the verge of breaking at every shot, the two to one ratio does not seem, to me, to be a practical ratio to use in making bows. Hamilton agrees with me and says that the practical bow draw ratio should be higher than two to one.

I believe we can arrive at a practical bow length to arrow length ratio by using the long experience of the Cherokee bowyers. As I stated above, many Cherokee D bows five to 5-1/2 feet long are used to shoot arrows 28 inches long. A 60 inch bow shooting a 28 inch arrow would give a ratio of 2.14 to 1, which I consider more practical than the two to one ratio. The difference between 2.14 and 2 does not seem like much but, in bow length, it makes the difference between a 60 inch bow and a 56 inch bow which is a very significant difference.

The six foot English longbow shooting a 28 inch arrow would have a ratio of 2.57 to 1 which, according to our "ideal" ratio, would be a rather inefficient bow.

Now that we have compared the Cherokee D bow with the English longbow, we need to compare the Cherokee D and handle bows. For this comparison, the bow length to arrow length ratio is not much help because the non-bending handle section is part of the length of the bow but is not part of the bending limbs of the bow. The handle bow has a handle section 10 to 12 inches long that does not bend while the D bow has no handle section and bends the entire length of the bow. Thus, if we compare a five foot D bow and a six foot handle bow, the length of the wood that is actually bending is about five feet in each type of bow. Obviously, we need to devise a different way to compare these two types of bows.

I devised a method which I have found useful for comparing the D bow and handle bow. I compare what I call the "bending radius" of each type of bow. If we analyze the bending of the two types of bows (Figures 9-4 and 9-5), the arc of the D bow, at a draw length of 28 inches, forms part of a circle whose radius is approximately 28 inches. The handle bow must be analyzed with two circles, one for each limb because the handle section is not bending. At a draw length of 28 inches, the arc of each limb of the handle bow forms part of a circle whose radius is approximately 29.8 inches.

The difference in the bending radius of the D bow and the bending radius of the handle bow is 1.8 inches. If we divide 1.8 inches by either radius (28 or 29.8), the difference is about 6%. Although the length of bending wood is the same in each bow, the wood in the handle bow is stressed less than the wood in the D bow. We should be able to reduce the length of

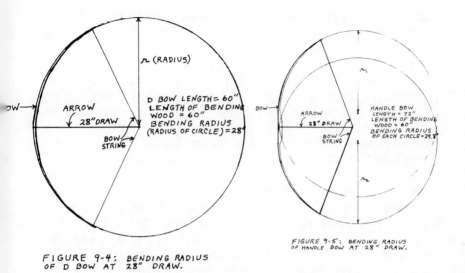

FIGURE 9-4: BENDING RADIUS
OF D BOW AT 28" DRAW.

FIGURE 9-5: BENDING RADIUS
OF HANDLE BOW AT 28" DRAW.

DRAW LENGTH (inches)	D BOW (inches)	HANDLE BOW (inches)
30	64	73
29	62	70
28	60	68
27	58	65
26	56	63
25	54	61
24	51	58
23	49	56
22	47	53

Figure 9-6: Minimum Length of D Bow
and Handle Bow for Specified Draw
Length

the handle bow until its bending radius is near that of the D bow, thereby approaching the stress level of the D bow and making the handle bow more efficient.

A six foot handle bow shooting a 28 inch arrow, gives a ratio of 2.57 to 1. Allowing for the 6% differential in bending radius, would reduce the ratio for a handle bow to 2.42 to 1. This reduces the length of the handle bow needed to shoot a 28 inch arrow from 72 inches to 68 inches. At this ratio, the handle bow should be stressed about the same and have about the same efficiency as the five foot D bow.

Therefore, if you plan to make a D bow that bends over its entire length, determine its minimum length by multiplying your arrow length by 2.14 and round the product to the nearest half inch. For example, a 28 inch arrow would require a D bow 60 inches long (28x2.14=60). For a handle bow, multiply your arrow length by 2.42. For a 28 inch arrow, your handle bow length would be 68 inches. The minimum lengths of D and handle bows for different draw lengths are shown in Figure 9-6. At the minimum length, your bow will be near maximum efficiency but also highly stressed so I recommend that you make your bow two or three inches longer than the minimum. It will still shoot with good efficiency and it should last longer because there will be less stress on the limbs.

CHAPTER 10

BOW WEIGHT

Another thing you should decide before you start carving is the approximate draw weight you want your finished bow to be. The width, thickness and length of the bow limbs will determine the weight of your bow. In Chapter 16, I have provided dimensions which will give you bows of different weights.

The heavier your bow, the faster it will shoot an arrow and the better penetration you will get. Generally, your bow should be as heavy as you can handle, even if you have to work out some to build up your muscles before you can handle it. A Cherokee bow of 40 pounds draw weight can be used to hunt deer but I feel more confident of adequate penetration with a heavier bow, especially if I am hunting game that is larger than whitetailed deer.

I hunt mule deer and elk with a 70 to 80 pound bow, whitetailed deer with a 50 to 60 pound bow and small game witha 40-45 pound bow. Actually, I enjoy shooting the light bows more than the heavy ones.

Another factor you must consider is the difference between a longbow and a compound bow. Just because you have been shooting a 60 pound compound does not mean you can easily handle a 60 pound longbow. With the compound, you only have to pull the 60 pounds for an instant as the bow "breaks over" and then you only have to hold a fraction of that weight at full draw. With the longbow, the weight increases as you draw the arrow until you hold the peak weight at full draw. That is one reason that longbow shooters pulling heavy bows often hold for a very short time at full draw.

If you make your bow a little too heavy you can always take off some of the weight by rasping down the belly of the bow a little. If you make it too light, you can increase the weight by cutting off the tips of the limbs and carving new nocks. Taking an inch off each end will increase the draw weight about five pounds.

Finally, let me caution you again about taking your time in making your bow. Beginning bowmakers are often disappointed to find that their finished bow doesn't draw as heavy as they had wanted. This happens when they get in a hurry and take off too much wood in one spot on a limb and then have to thin the rest of the bow to match the thin spot.

CHAPTER 11

FINDING AND CUTTING THE TREE

Locating osage orange trees is easier than finding one suitable for making a bow. In eastern Oklahoma, where I cut my osage orange, I estimate that about one tree out of a hundred is suitable for making bow "staves". A stave is a piece of wood about two inches square and four to six feet long which is split out of a log and used for making a bow. A higher percentage of trees, perhaps 10 to 20 percent, is suitable for making "billets", half the length of staves, two of which are spliced together to make a bow. After the billets are joined, the making of a bow proceeds the same as for a stave.

I watch for "good" trees while I am hunting during the year. For staves, I look for a tree trunk about six feet long, straight and without limbs. Any small limbs growing from the main trunk go completely into the heart of the trunk and complicate the making of a bow. For making bows, the trunk should be at least four to five inches in diameter at the small end. A diameter of eight to twelve inches is ideal. Sometimes a large limb from a big tree is suitable but I prefer the trunk of the tree. For billets, I look for the same things that make a good stave except the piece needs to be only about three feet long.

I return to cut the tree during the winter while the tree is dormant. I cut the tree with a saw to get the maximum length staves or billets, preferably six and one half to seven feet long for staves and 38 to 40 inches long for billets. The extra length allows for some trimming later, when I make the bow, so I can get a finished bow length of about six feet. An osage orange log seven feet long and a foot in diameter is quite heavy so you will probably need help carrying it out of the woods.

The old bowyers pay close attention to the moon and other signs, some of which are secret and shared with no "Yonega" (white man). One belief is that the tree should be cut when the moon is between its last quarter and its first quarter, and the nearer to the dark of the moon the better. It should never be cut when the moon is full. Also, the log must be marked as to which end grew up and which end was near the ground. The bow must be made so that the top of the bow is from the top of the log and the bottom from the bottom. If the bow is made upside down, it will never shoot accurately.

I, being educated and all, came to doubt some of the old ways so, as a test,

I deliberately cut a tree during the full
moon and made the bow upside down. The
results reestablished my belief in the
wisdom of the old bowyers. The only way I
could hit anything with that damned bow
was to shoot it while hanging upside down
in a tree on a dark night. Since the bow
was useless for anything except hunting
bats, I gave it to a man I don't like.

FIGURE 11-1: Osage
Orange in Winter.

FIGURE 11-2: Close-
up of Osage Orange.

FIGURE 11-3: Osage Orange Logs.

CHAPTER 12

SPLITTING THE LOG AND REMOVING THE BARK

The first thing that I do with the log, when I get it home, is split it and remove the bark. Splitting the log will reveal if the grain of the wood is straight or twisted and removing the bark will reveal knots and flaws in the wood that were not visible before. I then make the decision whether the piece of wood is suitable for making bows. Actually, almost any piece of osage orange will make a bow but, if the grain is too crooked or the wood has too many knots, making a bow may require more work than I want to do.

Another reason to remove the bark from the log is to prevent damage from insect larvae during the seasoning process. There are usually wood borer eggs under the bark that will hatch out worms that will bore into the log (Figure 12-1).

Usually, they make holes only in the softer sapwood, which I remove when I make the bow, but sometimes they bore into the heartwood and ruin the wood for making a bow. By removing the bark, I eliminate most of the worms. I don't have to be too careful when removing the bark; if I remove some sapwood, it doesn't matter, but I am careful not to cut into the darker heartwood (Figure 12-2).

I split the log with steel wedges and sledge hammer (Figure 12-3). A small log, four or five inches in diameter is split in half and, if I am lucky, will make two bow staves; one from each half. A log eight inches in diameter is quartered and might make four staves. I might get as many as six or eight staves out of a large log. I have had little success splitting the logs by sawing with a chain saw or at a saw mill. Often, the wood grain of the log has a twist in it. Splitting with wedges follows the twisting grain and, if it isn't too bad, I can remove the twist later with heat. On the other hand, a saw cuts across the grain and the bow which is made from that stave may break.

Before you split your log, look at the log and decide on the best position to start the wedges. Small limbs or imperfections in the wood only go through to the center of the log so, by splitting the log in a certain way, you may be able to obtain a good stave from one half and leave all the imperfections in the other half. Also, look at the end of the log so that you can see the growth rings in the wood. Often, the center "pith" is not in the center of the log because one side of the trunk has grown faster than the other. Position your wedges so that the split goes through the off-center pith and still

FIGURE 12-1: Borer
Holes.

FIGURE 12-2: Remov-
ing Bark.

FIGURE 12-3a: FIGURE 12-3b:
        Splitting Log Into Staves.

splits the log into equal halves.

If the half-log you split off is more than four inches wide, measured across the curved surface at the smaller end, you can probably split it in half and obtain two staves. If the pith is off center, however, you will probably have to split the half-log with a band saw to obtain two usable staves. Of course, you can split it with your wedges and sledge but often one of the staves will split off thin so that it can't be used. If the log was short and you plan to make billets, the half-log is split or sawed in two to form two billets, which you will later splice together to form a stave.

If you have time, you can partially carve out your bow while the wood is green and then let it cure a few months or years before tillering and shooting it. In the olden days, every Indian warrior kept bow staves, greased and in various stages of carving and seasoning, in his lodge to be worked on at his leisure. If you don't have time to do more than remove the bark, just put the log in a dry place to season until you need it.

A final word of advice: don't abandon the project at this point because the stave you split out is crooked or twisted and looks like it could never be made into a bow. Like baby swans, most osage orange staves look like ugly ducklings at this point but, with patient work, you will transform that ugly, useless piece of wood into a beautiful, functional work of art.

CHAPTER 13

SEASONING AND CURING THE WOOD

The strength and endurance of a self bow is greatly influenced by the seasoning and curing of the wood from which the bow is made. We will define seasoning as the controlled drying of the wood over a span of time. Curing will refer to using chemical and physical processes to improve the quality of the wood beyond mere drying, to prevent drying beyond the desired moisture content of the wood, and to protect the wood from moisture after it has seasoned. As the wood is seasoned and cured, it will increase in strength and resilience. However, if the wood dries out too much, it loses its resilience, becomes brittle and is more likely to break.

The wood should be seasoned by air drying at normal temperatures rather than kiln drying. Kiln drying makes the wood too brittle so that a bow made from it will probably break. The bowyer attempts to get the moisture content of the wood just right; less than the amount in green wood but not dried out so much that the wood becomes brittle. Therefore, the fresh cut wood is allowed to season, or slowly dry out, for a time, depending on where it is stored, the average humidity of the air, temperature and other factors. I believe the maximum resiliency of osage orange wood is achieved at a moisture content of about 15%. For comparison purposes, kiln dried laminations for building laminated bows are dried to about 8% moisture content.

I hasten to add that I do not check the moisture content of my bow wood and neither do you have to check yours in order to make a good bow. If you let the wood air dry, using the methods I suggest, the moisture content of the wood will be about right. If it is a little too moist when you make your bow, it will continue to season and your bow may gain in draw weight. If the wood seems too dry when you work it (which isn't likely) soak it in water for a week or so.

After I have removed the bark and split out my staves as described in the previous chapter, I coat the ends of the staves or billets with paraffin to control the rate of moisture loss (Figure 13-1). The wood will lose moisture about fifteen times faster from the ends of the grain than from either the edge or flat of the grain. Even with the paraffin, this rapid drying may cause weather cracks to appear at the ends of the staves. Since I usually cut the staves or billets longer than I need, I can cut off the few inches that are badly cracked and still have plenty of length.

A few years ago, as a further preventative against the wood drying too fast, I began seasoning my staves and billets in a dry cave where the temperature is constant and the air somewhat humid. But for years, I seasoned staves under my front porch with acceptable results. It is best to keep the staves off the ground and out of direct sunlight.

As the stave seasons and loses moisture, small season cracks may appear in the white sapwood and may extend down into the heartwood (Figure 13-2). You can probably avoid some of these cracks by removing the sapwood while the stave is still green. I usually do not have time to remove the sapwood while I am gathering wood in the winter so I season most of my wood with the sapwood on and deal with the weather cracks later. Since these cracks run parallel with the grain of the wood, they usually cause no problem with the making or shooting of the bow. Also, by removing a few layers of heartwood grain, I can often remove the cracks completely. To prevent season cracks in the wood, You may want to grease or oil your entire stave during the seasoning process as did the Indian warriors of old. I have not completely solved the problem of season cracks in my own wood and I am still experimenting with different methods of preventing them.

You will be eager to finish your bow and shoot it but, if you are to have a good bow, you cannot rush the seasoning process. I have shot bows seasoned only three months but I strongly recommend at least six months of seasoning before you shoot your bow and a year is even better. Since I keep a large supply of osage orange wood and replenish it yearly, I make my bows from wood that has seasoned three to five years. If you don't want to wait that long, buy or trade for a piece of seasoned wood and make a bow to use until the wood you cut has seasoned.

The curing process involves putting something on the wood to keep the moisture content at a desirable level as well as to toughen and protect the wood (Figure 13-3). The first thing that comes to mind is a finish of some type such as varnish but the old-time Cherokee bowyers did not have varnish and found something better. They rubbed bear oil on the bow and warmed it so that it penetrated the wood. Warm hog lard is much like bear oil and today's Cherokees find it works well. The oil holds the moisture content of the wood as varnish would but does something the varnish won't. When it penetrates the wood, the oil makes the wood tough and very resistant to breaking, beyond what mere moisture content will account for. I do not know the scientific explanation for it, but it works.

Many other things are used by Cherokee bowyers for curing bow wood. Richard McLemore, the Cherokee who made my first bow, used to rub his bows with a rag dipped in turpentine. I guess it worked because he had an old, almost black, bow that had been in his family for more than a hundred years. He shot it sometimes and it was still strong. Bill Cabbagehead, another Cherokee bowyer, rubs vegetable cooking oil on his bows and Bill's father used to soak staves in a pond to cure them. Terry Birdtail shoots an old black bow he says was cured with used motor oil!

66

FIGURE 13-1: Seal-
ing Ends of Stave.

FIGURE 13-2: Sea-
son Crack in Stave.

FIGURE 13-3: Oil Finishes.

Alex England, one of my Cherokee teachers and a recognized master bowyer, told me he has used kerosene to keep the wood from weather cracking and he rubs his finished bows with hog lard.

There used to be many white bowyers around the United States who were famous for their beautiful self bows and, like the Cherokee bowyers, they each had their favorite curing method for the wood. My friend, Glenn St.Charles of Seattle, who is an old-time bowyer of considerable fame as founder of the Pope and Young Club uses teak oil on the yew-wood bows that he makes and it seems to work well on osage orange as well. Another old-time bowyer, Jim Glendening of California, told me he prefers a tung oil finish on osage orange bows.

After your bow is completed, you need to rub in a fresh application of grease or oil fairly often, perhaps every week or two if you are using the bow a lot, and two or three times a year if the bow is stored. I store my finished bows in the dry cave with my supply of staves and billets since they dry out too much inside my house.

If you find an old bow that someone has had stored for a long time, you need to give it special treatment. It is common for someone to find such a bow, string it, pull it and see it break! A bow that has been stored a long time inside a house will dry out to the point that the wood becomes brittle. If you want to shoot such a bow, you need to restore the moisture content of the wood. If the bow has a varnish type finish on it, scrape or sand the finish off and then soak the bow in water for a week or two before you try to string and shoot it.

CHAPTER 14

SPLICING BILLETS

Osage orange bow staves, long enough to make a good bow, are hard to find so you may decide to use billets instead of a stave. Each billet is only about three feet long and, therefore, much easier to find than pieces for staves. The billets are spliced together in the middle and then you proceed with making your bow as if you were using a stave. I suppose it is possible to make a D bow using billets but I always make a handle bow when using them because the thickness, width, and non-bending of the handle all contribute to a strong splice joint.

Before I learned to make a fishtail splice, I spliced my billets with a section of pipe (Figure 14-1). I made the pipe splice using a 4 inch long piece of thin-walled steel pipe that was about 1

1/4 inch in diameter. I whittled the ends of the billets down until they snugly slipped into the pipe to a depth of about two inches and the two flat ends met in the middle of the pipe. Then I liberally coated the ends of the billets with glue, socked them into the pipe and let them set. The resulting splice was very strong and usually solid but even if the limbs were slightly loose in the pipe, they locked solidly in place when the bow was strung and the bow shot as well as if it were made from a solid stave. After the bow was complete and tillered, I shaped the handle the way I wanted it with plastic wood and covered it with a leather grip so that the pipe was completely hidden.

However, a glued fishtail joint is better than a piece of pipe and is not as hard to do as you might think. It helps to have a band saw but you can use a fine toothed hand saw or back saw if you have no band saw. Basically, you will mark and saw out two fingers on the end of one billet and three fingers on the end of the other billet (Figures 14-2 & 14-3). You will then put glue on all surfaces, slip the fingers together and clamp the joint until the glue hardens (Figure 14-4).

I have had some problems getting glue to hold on osage orange wood because the wood contains an oil that prevents the glue from sticking. So I treat the wood with a lye water solution before I glue it. You can buy lye in granule form at the grocery store. Lye is dangerous so read the directions on the can and be careful. I always wear goggles when I am working with lye water. Dissolve about a tablespoon of lye in a pint of cold water and pour it over the parts you intend to

FIGURE 14-1:
Pipe Splice.

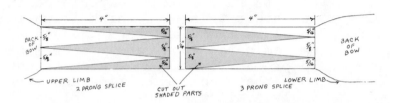

FIGURE 14-2: DIMENSIONS OF FISHTAIL SPLICE

FIGURE 14-3: Splice
Ready to Glue.

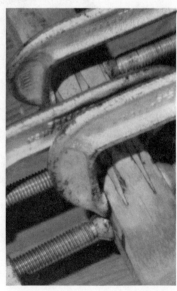

FIGURE 14-4: Clamps
on Glued Joint.

glue. Then rinse the wood by pouring
boiling water over it. After the wood
dries (you can speed it up with a blow
dryer), apply the glue and clamp the
pieces together.

There are many glues that will work
well in holding the joint. I have used
Elmer's Carpenter's Glue, an epoxy glue
called Wil-Hold and a slow setting epoxy
by Duro. I have not tried hide glue for
joining billets but, from my experience in
using it on other things, I think it would
hold. The glues that have been developed
for gluing laminated wood and fiberglass
bows would probably work but I don't use
them because they require heating and are
not as widely available as the glues I
use.

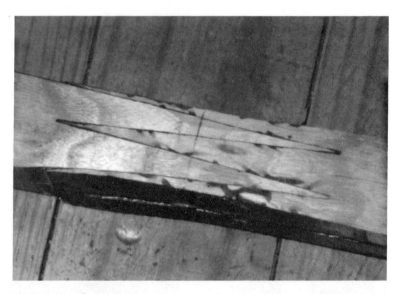

FIGURE 14-5: Completed Fishtail Joint.

CHAPTER 15

REMOVING THE SAPWOOD AND FOLLOWING THE GRAIN

If you are to successfully make a bow, you must have an understanding of the wood. Looking at the cut end of an osage orange log (Figure 15-1), the outermost layer is the bark. The next layer beneath the bark is the sapwood which is about 1/4 to 1/2 inch thick and whitish in color. Beneath the sapwood is the yellow heartwood made up of the growth rings which appear as a pattern of concentric light and dark circles. Each ring is the end of a layer or "grain" of wood which extends through the length of the log. I will refer to these as "grain layers".

The trunk of the tree grew in layers, adding two new grain layers of wood around the trunk each year. Each "annual ring" or "growth ring" consists of a light

colored ring and a dark colored ring. A
light colored growth ring and
corresponding grain layer is porous,
formed from large cells in the spring when
growth conditions are more favorable. A
dark ring and grain layer is more dense
and smooth, formed from smaller cells in
summer when growth conditions are less
favorable.

Your understanding of the nature of
these grain layers is critical in making a
good bow. The "back" of your completed
bow will be formed by one of the dark,
dense, grain layers (Figure 15-1).

Most Cherokee bowyers remove all the
sapwood and make the bow entirely from the
heartwood although I have seen osage
orange bows with some sapwood left on that
shot all right. But I always remove the
sapwood.

After removing the sapwood, the next
step in making a bow is to carefully
follow a single dense grain layer of
heartwood over the entire back of the bow.
Following a single grain layer is
difficult but necessary if you are to make
a bow that is least likely to break. This
grain layer will be the "back" of your
completed bow. Remember, the side that is
away from you when you shoot the bow is
the "back" while the " belly" is the side
toward you when you shoot it (You might
want to refer back to Figure 8-1). If you
visualize it inside the log, the back of
the bow faces out toward the bark while
the belly faces toward the center of the
log (Figure 15-1).

Many years ago, Richard McLemore, my
Cherokee teacher, told me, as he watched
my frustrated efforts to follow a grain
layer, "Listen to the wood! He will talk
to you." Richard was right! If I

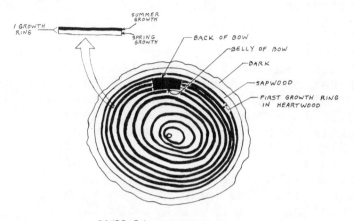

SUMMER GROWTH

1 GROWTH RING

SPRING GROWTH

BACK OF BOW

BELLY OF BOW

BARK

SAPWOOD

FIRST GROWTH RING IN HEARTWOOD

FIGURE 15-1: CROSS SECTION OF OSAGE ORANGE LOG SHOWING POSITION OF BOW IN LOG.

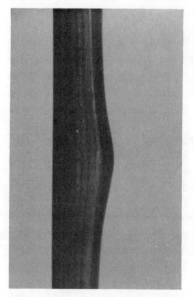

FIGURE 15-2: Hump Where Grain Goes Over Knot.

FIGURE 15-3: Working the Back of the Stave.

listened closely, I could hear different sounds as the draw knife cut through the different grain layers. Also, if I looked closely, I could see the large cells, like a tiny honeycomb, in the porous, light colored layers. I learned to watch and listen as I cut through the porous grain layer to the denser, smooth layer below.

If there is a knot in the wood, there will be a hump in the wood there and the grain must be followed over the hump (Figure 15-2). If you cut off the hump to make it smooth with the rest of the bow surface, the bow may break there when you shoot it. The hump will not affect the shooting or durability of the bow. An osage orange bow that has no humps or other imperfections is seldom seen and most connoisseurs of primitive bows consider the imperfections as part of their beauty as opposed to the sterile precision of a factory made bow. I once saw a picture of a self bow in the Fred Bear archery museum which was literally covered with humps. I marvelled at the patience of the bowyer who brought forth that work of art from a knotty and twisted piece of wood.

But let's get to work on the back of your bow. Use a draw knife to remove the bark if it hasn't already been removed. Then remove the sapwood down to the yellow heartwood. Then, starting at the end of the stave nearest to you and pulling the draw knife toward you (Figure 15-3), carefully cut away thin shavings of wood. Your goal is to locate a single dense grain layer and follow it over the entire back of the bow. The draw knife will cut best if you turn the beveled edge of the blade toward the wood as you draw the knife toward you. Of course, you need to have the stave fastened in a vice or shaving horse to hold it.

As you cut with the draw knife, watch for the large cells in the porous layers and listen for the grating sound the blade makes as it cuts into those layers. Beneath each porous layer lies a dense, smooth layer which is the summer growth and one of those is the layer you want for the back of your bow. I usually remove two or three grain layers before choosing one to be the back of my bow.

Osage orange wood often has the tendency to "dig in" as you cut it with a draw knife so that, instead of removing a thin shaving, a thick chunk is torn from the wood. This is common around knots and when working on the belly of the bow. When the wood shows the tendency to dig in, it is wise to stop using the draw knife on that place and use your wood rasp or scraper instead. Especially when following a grain layer over a knot on the back, I always use a vixen file, fine toothed rasp or scraper instead of a draw knife to prevent digging into the wood.

I have devised a method for following a single layer of grain in the wood that works well for me (Figure 15-4). I remove the first two dense grain layers of heartwood and the porous layer beneath each and leave the third dense layer. As each of the two dense grain layers with their underlying porous layers are removed, it makes a line across the back of the bow where the edge of the grain overlaps the grain layer beneath (Figure 15-5). The lines indicating the edge of the grain layers will progress up the bow as the layers are removed.

To simplify the following description, I will only speak of removing the dense

77

layer but you should understand that I also mean the removal of the porous layer just beneath the dense layer.

Holding the stave in the shaving horse or vise and beginning on the end nearest to me, I remove the first dense grain layer from a few inches of the stave with the draw knife. Then I remove a few inches more of that first grain layer, and continue the process until I have removed the first grain layer from about 12 inches of the stave. As I work the grain layer off, I can see the line which marks the edge of the grain layer moving away from me and that line serves as a guide to how far I have gone.

Next, I remove the next grain layer that I exposed when I took off the first layer. I work the second grain layer edge line back until it is within an inch or two of the line marking the first layer I removed. I now have two lines to guide me. By continuing to follow these lines in removing the two grain layers from the entire back of the bow, I have one continuous layer for the back of my bow.

You can remove as many grain layers as you want before choosing one to serve as the back of your bow. For instance, if there are some shallow weather cracks or worm holes in the wood, you may be able to eliminate them by taking off a few more grain layers. If you inadvertently cut through the grain layer you intend to use for the back, you must start again and take the whole layer off down to the next grain layer.

Following a grain layer can be a frustrating experience for a person from today's time-oriented world. But, when you have succeeded in following one grain layer over the entire bow, you will have

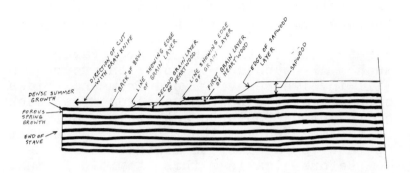

DIRECTION OF CUT WITH DRAW KNIFE
"BACK" OF BOW
LINE SHOWING EDGE OF GRAIN LAYER
SECOND GRAIN LAYER OF HEARTWOOD
LINE SHOWING EDGE OF GRAIN LAYER
FIRST GRAIN LAYER OF HEARTWOOD
EDGE OF SAPWOOD LAYER
SAPWOOD
DENSE SUMMER GROWTH
POROUS SPRING GROWTH
END OF STAVE

FIGURE 15-4: HERRIN METHOD OF FOLLOWING GRAIN

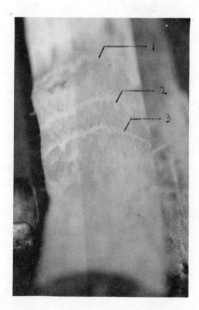

FIGURE 15-5: Lines Made By Edges of Grain Layers. Three lines are visable. #1 is edge of sapwood. #2 & #3 are first two layers of heartwood.

passed a test of patience, perseverance, and understanding which few others could pass.

Once you have succeeded in following one grain layer over the entire surface of the bow, you can remove any tool marks with your scraper and sandpaper, being careful not to thin the grain layer too much. All subsequent work on your bow will involve removing wood from the sides or belly of the bow, never from the back of the bow. Don't forget this--you went to too much work on that back to mess it up later by a careless mistake!

Before leaving this topic, I must address the fact that some Cherokee bows are seen that show little or no attempt to follow a single grain layer on the back of the bow. I would like to tell you that such bows always break but, dammit, they don't always break. I would like to tell you that bows with a single grain layer over the back never break but, dammit again, sometimes they do break. I can tell you, in truth, that the probability of breakage is far less in a correctly made bow with one grain layer over the whole back. Also, in my opinion, a bow that does not follow the grain on the back shows poor craftsmanship and shows me a bowyer that is ignorant, lazy, or more interested in time or money than making a good bow. Whether you are making or buying a primitive bow, you can have an inferior bow for much less than a good bow will cost in time or money but you are better off spending the extra time or money to get a good bow. Roger Ascham, author of <u>Toxophilus</u>, shared my opinion in 1545 when he wrote to English archers, "For a good bow twise paide for is better than an ill bowe once broken."

CHAPTER 16

MARKING AND ROUGHING-OUT THE BOW

The dimensions of several different types and weights of bows are shown in Figures 16-1 and 16-2. You can use the dimensions to mark-out the approximate shape and size of your bow before you start to work the wood. Of course, the final weight of the bow will vary somewhat depending on factors over which you have little control, such as the nature of the wood itself, so that two bows of exactly the same dimensions and of the same wood may have slightly different draw weights. Your best plan is to slowly remove the wood as you get close to your final dimensions and frequently test the bow weight. If your final bow is too heavy, you can always remove more wood but, if it is too light, you can't put wood back on.

Sight down the back of your stave, the

DIMENSIONS OF BOWS SHOWN IN FIGURES 16-1 AND 16-2: Bows are numbered from top to bottom. Draw weights are at 28 inch draw except bow 5 which is at 22 inch draw. Approximate cross sectional shape of all bow limbs is rectangular. Bows 1-4 are made of osage orange, bow 5 is made of black locust.

(1) D bow. Draw weight: 65 pounds.:Length between nocks: 71 inches. Width of limbs at widest point: 1-9/16 inch. Thickness of limbs at thickest point: 5/8 inch. Width of tip at nock: 1-1/16 inch. Thickness of tip at nock: 7/16 inch.

(2) D bow. Draw weight: 50 pounds. Length between nocks: 64 inches. Width of limbs at widest point: 1-5/8 inch. Thickness of limbs at thickest point: 9/16 inch (Back of bow is somewhat rounded so thickness at edge of limbs is about 1/4 inch). Width of tip at nock: 1-1/16 inch. Thickness of tip at nock: 5/16 inch.

(3) Handle bow. Draw weight: 55 pounds. Length between nocks: 69 inches. Width of limbs at widest point: 1-9/16 inch. Thickness of limbs at thickest point (excluding handle): 7/16 inch. Width of tip at nock: 13/16 inch. Thickness of tip at nock: 3/8 inch.

(4) Handle bow. Draw weight 45 pounds. Length between nocks: 71 inches. Width of limbs at widest point: 1-3/8 inch. Thickness of limbs at thickest point (excluding handle): 9/16 inch. Width of tip at nock: 11/16 inch. Thickness of tip at nock: 1/4 inch.

(5) Sioux style horse bow. Draw weight 55 pounds at 22 inch draw. Length between nocks: 54 inches. Width of limbs at widest point: 1-3/8 inch. Thickness of limbs at thickest point (excluding handle): 1/2 inch. Width of tip at nock: 3/4 inch. Thickness of tip at nock: 5/16 inch.

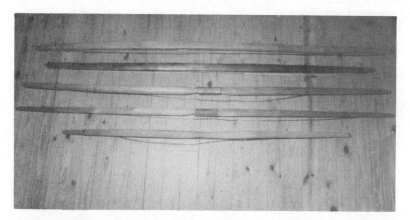

FIGURE 16-1: View of Backs of Five Bows.

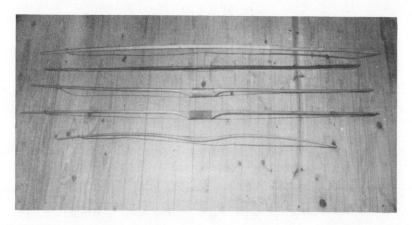

FIGURE 16-2: View of Sides of Five Bows.

side you removed the sapwood from, and see if it appears straight from end to end. If it looks straight, mark a center line down the back of the stave from end to end. I use a chalk line to make the mark and then go over that with pencil. If you can avoid a flaw or knot in the wood by marking the line to either side of the center of the stave and still have room for your bow, do it, but don't angle your center line across your stave. The center line should pretty well follow the way the wood grew.

If your stave curves to the side, don't mark a straight center line the entire length of the stave but, instead, mark a curved center line that follows the curve of your stave. Later, after you have removed some wood from the sides and belly of the bow, you will be able to remove the curve by heating the wood.

If you wish, you can determine the length of the bow and cut off any extra length from your stave. I sometimes leave an inch or two extra on each end and cut it off later. I don't know why, but it makes me feel better. Measure the length, divide by two and mark the center of your bow.

If you plan to have a handle, mark it out next on the back of the stave (Figure 16-3). Mark the arrow-rest 1 1/4 inch above the center line and the bottom of the handle 3 inches below the center line for a total handle length of 4 1/4 inches. If you prefer, you can mark an arrow rest only on one side so you can cut the sight window deep enough to approach a center shot bow. I make an arrow rest on both sides so the bow can be shot either right or left handed. I do it because it is traditional and I think it looks better.

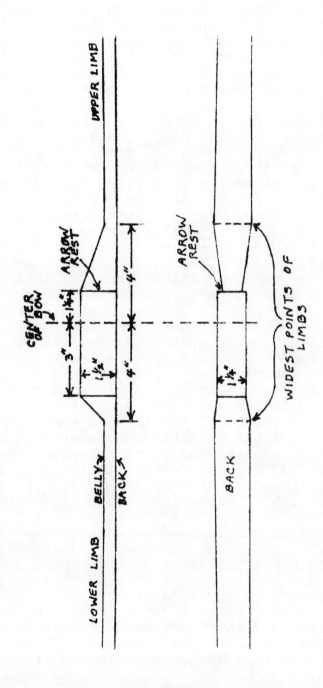

FIGURE 16-3: DIMENSIONS OF HANDLE.

Next, mark-out the width and general shape of the limbs on the back of the stave. You may be able to use a straight-edge to mark the lines but, if you cut on the straight line from near your handle to the tips of your limbs, you may find it is too narrow in the center of the limbs. Leave some extra width on the limbs for later shaping by eye.

Now you are ready to remove wood from the sides of your bow down to the lines you have marked. I usually use an axe initially (Figure 16-4) and then, when I am getting down close to the lines, I use a draw knife and finally a rasp.

After you have removed the wood from the sides of the bow, lay the stave on its side and mark the raised handle section, if you plan to have one, and the thickness of the limbs. My handle design differs somewhat from the design of some of the old time bowyers such as Howard Hill. I want you to be aware of this so you can choose the design you prefer. The non-bending sections of their handles were more in the lower limb with the result that the bending portion of the lower limb was about two inches shorter than the bending portion of the upper limb. Because of this difference in length, the upper limb did not bend the same as the lower limb. This practice was used among most of the English-tradition bowyers who claimed it gave better balance to the bow.

The tradition among most Indian tribes in North America was that the bow handle was made in the center of the bow and the limbs were of equal length and this is the tradition I follow. Actually, I have shot and compared many bows made on each design and I can tell no difference in "balance" (whatever that is) or performance of the

FIGURE 16-4: Roughing-Out the Bow.

bows. Reginald Laubin, a bowyer who makes
sinew-backed bows, has also found no
difference in shooting the two designs of
bows. So, I see no reason for limbs of
unequal length and I build the non-bending
sections of my handles in the center of
the bow so that both limbs bend the same.

My "centered" design has a couple of
advantages over the "off-center" design.
Because the limbs bend the same, my bows
are easier to tiller (get the limbs to
bend the same amount). In addition, the
bending radii and stresses of my bows are
the same on both limbs. In the off center
design, the bending radius of the lower
limb is shorter than the bending radius of
the upper limb making the lower limb more
stressed. This can be seen in the fact
that the lower limb of those bows often
shows more string follow than does the
upper limb. I believe this uneven stress
on the two limbs could shorten the life of
the bow.

87

I try to keep the non-bending handle section as short as I can and I usually make it about eight inches long. On the side of the stave, I mark lines four inches above and below the center line (Figure 16-3). Those lines define where the raised handle section will drop to the level of the belly of the bow. Next, I mark the belly of the bow, leaving extra wood to remove later during tillering. Then, I use first an axe and then a draw knife to remove the wood from the belly of the bow down to the marks I made.

If you are building a D bow, just mark a line to define the belly of the bow and remove wood down to the line.

I have mentioned this before but it is important enough to bear repeating. You may find that your draw knife tends to "dig in" and tear out big pieces of wood as you work on the belly of the bow. When you encounter such a place, use your rasp to remove the wood.

You are finally getting your stave down to where it is starting to look like a bow. But it may have some crooked places that you need to remove so our next chapter will deal with shaping your bow with heat.

CHAPTER 17

STRAIGHTENING WITH HEAT

You will be surprised how much you can affect the shape of your bow with heat and bending. You can straighten bends or twists in the bow and, once straightened, the bow will remain straight. If done carefully so the wood is not made brittle, the heating and bending does not seem to have any ill effect on the performance or life of the bow.

I do the straightening in my outdoor workshop under a tree in my front yard. I grease the bow with bacon drippings first. Then I heat the spot to be straightened over the burner of a Coleman stove, rotating the stave and moving it back and forth close over the flame to heat it evenly over an area on the stave from a few inches to a foot long. The wood must be hot before you bend it and sometimes the flame will scorch the wood but you can sand that off later. I test the temperature of the wood every few seconds with my palm and when the wood is too hot to hold, I bend it.

I use hot water to heat the bow wood for bending if the bend is severe and I feel I might make the wood too brittle heating it over direct flame. I have a three foot section of three inch steel pipe with a cap on one end (Figure 17-1). I prop the pipe at an angle, fill it with water and build a fire under it. I heat the bow, one limb at a time, in the boiling water and then bend the bow. Heating time varies from ten minutes to two hours depending on how much I want to bend the wood. The hot water removes the color from the surface of the wood but it can be restored by sanding.

To bend the wood, I put the heated spot on the stave in the fork of the tree by my workbench (Figure 17-2). Then I push or pull on the stave to bend it in the direction opposite the curve I am trying to remove. I bend it a little past the point where it is straight and hold it there until the wood cools or I get tired; two or three minutes. If I didn't straighten it enough, I do it again. Often, to straighten a long curve, I heat and bend several spots along the curve until the whole curve is straightened. A curve to the side, as you look down the back of the bow, is the hardest to straighten. A curve in the same plane in which the bow bends is easier to straighten. Many staves will bend "backward" a little when the stave is split from the log and I leave this backward bend to give the bow a natural reflex.

FIGURE 17-1: Heating the Stave in Boiling Water.

FIGURE 17-2: Bending the Heated Stave.

A long twist in the grain is usually easier to remove than a curve. To remove a twist in the stave, I clamp the stave in my vice on one side of the twist and put a pipe wrench on the other side of the twist, padding the vice and the wrench so their teeth don't cut into the wood. I heat the spot to be straightened with a propane torch and then straighten out the twist by pulling the pipe wrench in the correct direction.

You can use heat to bend the wood as well as straighten it. I have seen bows that were bent to form recurved tips or reflexed limbs. I have never tried to make such bows myself because I feel recurves detract from the purity of the Cherokee bow.

Now that your stave is straight, you may want to re-mark the center line and check the dimensions of your limbs to be sure they are what you want. When everything seems straight, you are ready to carve your nocks and begin tillering your bow.

CHAPTER 18

TILLERING THE BOW

Tillering is the process of getting your bow to bend correctly and is vital to making a bow that shoots well and won't break. Tillering is partly science and partly art. It will test your patience and your ability to recognize symmetry. I have used various methods of trying to analyze the bend of the limbs, such as marking off a grid on a large sheet and hanging it behind the bow, but I always wind up depending mostly on my eye and what looks right.

The tillering process will differ somewhat depending on the design of your bow. If you are building a D bow, tillering is the process of removing wood from the belly of the entire bow until the bend looks right and it pulls the weight you desire. For a handle bow, tillering is more complicated because you must remove wood from the two limbs until you have achieved three conditions: (1) each limb bends evenly along its entire length, (2) the two limbs bend equally and (3) the bow pulls the desired weight.

I use a three step process in tillering my handle bows.

(1) I bend the bow and observe where stiff spots appear in the limbs. Then I remove wood from the stiff spots until each limb bends evenly along its entire length.

(2) After the limbs are bending evenly, I bend the bow and determine if the two limbs are bending equally. If they aren't, I remove wood from the entire length of the stiffer limb until the two limbs bend equally.

(3) If the pull of the bow is too heavy, I remove wood from the entire length of both limbs until the desired weight is reached.

We will discuss these three steps in more detail later but there are some other things we need to cover first. And don't forget, in all these aspects of tillering, wood is removed only from the belly of the bow, never from the back of the bow.

Do not attempt to bend your bow the draw length of your arrow until the tillering process is almost completed. When you first start bending your bow at the beginning of the tillering, the limbs will always have some spots that are stiffer than others. If you try to bend the bow too much, the stiff spots will not bend, causing the weaker spots to bend too much which can cause that spot to break. The bending of your bow should take place in small increments or stages so that you do not place too much strain on any one place and risk breaking the bow. In other words, bend it only a little at first and remove some wood from the stiff spots. Then, bend it again and remove more wood from stiff spots. Continue until you have removed all the stiff spots and every inch of the limbs are bending. Only then should you draw your bow to the draw length of your arrows.

During the tillering you must be able to see the bow limbs bending and that can be difficult. You can try pulling the bow in front of a mirror or have someone else pull it so that you can observe how it bends but neither of these methods works very well. I have a tillering frame (Figure 18-1) with a shelf to support the bow handle and a cable through a pully to pull the string so I can stand back and look at the bow as I pull it. I can compare the bending of the two limbs and spot stiff spots in either limb.

Some bowyers use a board with pegs in it to tiller their bows. They put the bow in a notch in the top of the board and hook the string under a peg to hold it drawn so they can stand back and look at it. I like the simplicity of their apparatus but I still prefer a tillering frame because I can draw and release the tension more quickly and thus put less strain on the bow than if it were held drawn by a peg. Holding a self bow drawn for more than a few seconds puts a great strain on the wood, which is not good even when the bow is finished, but is particularly dangerous during tillering.

Now, let me take you through the tillering of a handle bow according to the three steps outlined above. You can easily modify the steps to work on a D bow if that is what you are making.

The first step involves finding and removing stiff spots so that the limbs bend evenly over their entire length. I start testing the bending of my bow by putting the tip on the floor and bending the bow a little with my hands as I watch and feel how it bends (Figure 18-2). Usually, it is so stiff at this point that I cannot bend it but I keep removing wood from the belly and retesting it until it bends and feels like it would pull 80 or 90 pounds. Then, I carve the nocks in the bow. Before we continue with the tillering, we need to briefly discuss bow nocks.

The bow nocks hold the bowstring at the ends of the bow (Figure 18-3). The traditional Cherokee D bow has deep nocks so that the tip of the bow above the nock forms a diamond shape. This design works best with a traditional string made of rawhide. The nocks are whittled with a pocket knife and the edges are left square rather than being rounded so that the edges of the nock help keep the rawhide string from slipping where it is tied on the lower nock. The sharp edges would quickly break a dacron string but the rawhide is very tough. If you plan to use a dacron string, you will want to round and smoothe the edges of the nocks.

The nocks for a handle bow are usually shallow since the tips of the handle bow are usually narrower than the tips of the D bow. If you plan to use a rawhide string on your handle bow, you will need to leave the tips a little wider and cut your nocks a little deeper. For a handle bow, I carve the nocks with a small round rasp. First, I rasp a groove across the

FIGURE 18-1: Tiller-
ing Frame.

FIGURE 18-2: First
Bending of the Bow.

FIGURE 18-4: Loose
String for Tillering.

FIGURE 18-3: Bow Nocks. English longbow,
Cherokee handle bow and Cherokee D bow.

back of the bow 1/2 inch from each tip.
Then I rasp a groove on each side of the
bow, beginning at the groove across the
back and sloping toward the handle (see
Figure 18-3). At this point in making
your bow, consider the nocks as temporary
ones for holding the string you will use
while tillering. You will probably have
to deepen the nocks a time or two as you
remove wood from the limbs.

I start the tillering process with a
string that is as long or longer than the
bow, looped or tied loosely in the nocks
(Figure 18-4). If you try to string your
bow with the length string you will use
later when your bow is finished, you will
bend your bow too much and you could break
your bow.

Now, back to step one in the tillering
process, the removal of stiff spots. I
put the loosely strung bow on my tillering
frame and pull the string enough to bend
the bow a litle while I look for stiff
spots in the bow (Figure 18-1). A stiff
spot will not bend as much as the rest of
the limb. I mark each stiff spot on the
belly of the bow with a felt-tip marker.
Then I remove the bow from the tillering
frame and rasp away wood from the marked
places (Figure 18-5). Then, I bend the
bow on the tillering frame and check again
for stiff spots, repeating the process
until each limb is bending evenly over its
entire length.

After I have the limbs bending evenly,
I pull the bow more on the tillering
frame, still watching for stiff spots,
until it is bending enough to be strung
with the string I will use for shooting
the finished bow. (Refer to Chapter 28 to
determine the length string you need.) At
this point, I remove the bow from the

tillering frame and string it full height for the first time.

STEP 2

This brings us to step two of the tillering process; getting the two limbs to bend the same. With the bow strung, I measure the distance from the string to the belly of the bow at intervals along each limb (Figure 18-6). For example, I measure down the string one foot from the tip of a limb and then measure the perpendicular distance from the string to the belly of the bow. Then, I repeat the procedure on the other limb. If the two measurements agree to within 1/4 inch or less, the limbs are bending about the

FIGURE 18-5: Rasping the Stiff Spots.

FIGURE 18-6: Checking Bend of Limbs.

FIGURE 18-7: Weighing the Bow.

same. I repeat the measurements at intervals from the tips down to the handle section and I can easily tell if one limb is stiffer and not bending as much at the other limb.

If you find that one limb is stiffer than the other, you remove wood from the stiffer limb until the limbs bend equally. You can either unstring the bow or leave it strung as you remove the wood from the belly. But whichever you do, after you remove wood, you must pull the bow a few times before you compare the limbs again. The removal of the wood doesn't seem to affect the stiffer limb until it is flexed and, if you don't flex it after each wood removal, you can easily remove too much wood and make that limb weaker than the other. After you have them bending equally, recheck for stiff spots in both limbs.

STEP 3

After you have the limbs bending evenly and equally and have drawn the bow back to your full arrow draw length, use a spring scale to test the weight of the bow at your draw length (Figure 18-7). If it is too heavy, remove wood evenly from the belly of both limbs until you get the weight you want. Then recheck to make sure the limbs are still bending evenly and equally. If, when you test the draw weight of your bow, it is too light, you can increase the weight by cutting off the tips of the limbs and carving new nocks. The weight should increase about five pounds for each inch taken off both tips. However, don't cut off so much that your bow is too short for your arrows causing you to overdraw and perhaps break your bow. A light bow is more fun than a broken bow.

CHAPTER 19

FINISHING THE BOW

All tool marks should be removed with your scraper and sandpaper and then use finer grades of sandpaper until you have a very smooth surface. I burnish my bows like the Northwest totum pole carvers burnished their carvings. They rubbed the wood with a flat, smooth stone to press in the grain of the wood and make a shiny smooth surface. You can use a little olive jar if you don't have a smooth stone. Just rub the wood with the side of the bottle.

If you choose to make a handle bow, the grip should be shaped to suit your preference. You can remove some wood with your rasp or build up some places with plastic wood. I usually carve a small piece of red cedar into the proper shape to make a shelf for an arrow rest on one

or both sides of the grip. After I get
the grip and arrow rest the way I want it,
I cut a piece of thin leather to go around
the grip and glue it in place (Figure
19-1).

Appy whatever finish you want; several
are discussed in Chapter 13. You may also
want to put your name on your bow, along
with the year it was made and its draw
weight. I use a woodburning tool to
inscribe this information on the handle of
my bows.

Your bow is finished and, if you have
done well, you have created a thing of
beauty as well as an efficient weapon.
With proper care, your children and
grandchildren will use and treasure "the
bow that Grandad made".

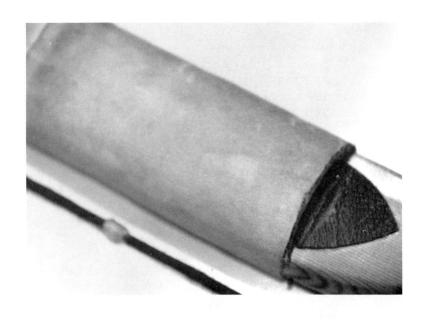

FIGURE 19-1: BOW GRIP

CHAPTER 20

ARROWS

Some of the old Cherokees used to say that anyone can make a bow but it takes great skill to make a good arrow. I think that saying was started by an arrow maker because no one who has ever succeeded in making a good bow would make such a statement. But it is certainly true that a lot of knowledge and skill is required to produce good arrows from raw materials found in nature. In many Indian tribes, the warriors made their own bows but obtained their arrows by trade from craftsmen who made arrows for the whole band.

The importance of arrow design was impressed on me by my good Cherokee friend, Lyman Vann. Lyman, who passed on to the happy hunting ground a few years ago, was a master bowyer and the best natural archer I ever knew. Since we both loved archery, we spent much time together, hunting rabbits and shooting cornstalks with our Cherokee bows and arrows.

Cornstalk shooting is a Cherokee sport in which you shoot arrows from a distance of about 100 yards at a target made of cornstalks (Figure 20-2). Since you get one point for each cornstalk your arrow penetrates, both accuracy and penetration are important in the game. Lyman usually won at the cornstalk shoots because he was accurate but also because his arrows penetrated deeper than anyone else's. His bow pulled only 45 or 50 pounds and I usually shot a bow pulling 65 or 70 pounds, yet he would average eight or nine stalks per hit while I averaged about six stalks per hit.

The difference was in the arrows. I know that my arrows were leaving my heavier bow with greater speed than Lyman's arrows were leaving his bow. But Lyman knew how to make a cornstalk arrow that would retain a great deal of its speed and energy over a distance of 100 yards which resulted in deeper penetration than my arrows which were evidently losing much of their speed and energy. I have experimented for years but have never been able to make an arrow that would equal Lyman's for combined accuracy and penetration. There is much more to making a good arrow than a straight stick and some feathers.

The old time arrowmakers were skilled but they were never sure that an arrow would shoot well until they finished it and shot it. Howard Hill talked about making up large numbers of arrows before a hunting trip and then shooting them at a

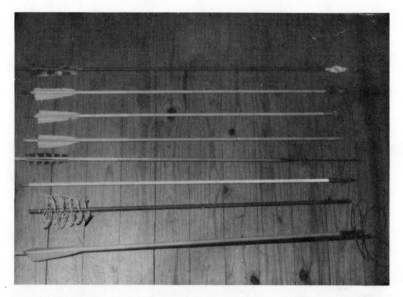

FIGURE 20-1: Eight Arrows for Various
Uses. Arrows are numbered from top to
bottom.
(1) Traditional Cherokee hunting arrow.
Feathers and flint point are tied to the
shaft with sinew.
(2) Hunting arrow with steel broadhead
point.
(3) Hunting arrow with small game point.
(4) Practice arrow with field point.
(5) Cornstalk shooting arrow with homemade
steel point. The long spike gives maximum
penetration in the target made of
cornstalks.
(6) Fish arrow with barbed steel point. No
fletching is necessary. Arrow and fish
are retrieved with an attached line.
(7) Flu-flu arrow with blunt tip for
shooting at things in the air or in trees.
The fletching slows the arrow so it
doesn't go far.
(8) Arrow for shooting at flying birds.
The four wire loops on the point increase
the chance of hitting the bird.

target to select the ones that shot
accurately while culling out the others.
As a boy, I always marked my arrows so I
would know which shot best and I reserved
my less accurate arrows for shots where I
was likely to lose the arrow. Today, I
can make arrows that I know will shoot
accurately before I ever try them and you
can do the same. The difference comes
from knowledge that the old time
arrowmakers did not have; a knowledge of
arrow spine or stiffness. We will discuss
this, in detail, in Chapter 22.

FIGURE 21-2: Cherokee Cornstalk Shoot.
Photo courtesy of Cherokee Nation.

CHAPTER 21

ARROW WOOD

The most widely used wood for making arrows is Port Orford Cedar which grows on the Pacific Coast in the Northwestern United States. Suppliers cut and mill the wood into arrow shafts which can be bought at archery shops around the country (Figure 21-1). The shafts are matched in diameter and spine (stiffness of the arrow) so they can be depended on to shoot accurately from your bow. This is the wood I use for most of my own arrows and what I would recommend that you use. However, we will discuss some other arrow woods in case you want to try some of them.

The traditional Cherokee cornstalk shooting arrows are made from black locust or osage orange wood (Figure 20-1). These woods are dense, heavy, hard, resilient and tough. A piece about three feet long is cut from the trunk of a tree and split many times until small bolts three feet long and about 1/2 inch square are produced. These are rounded with a knife and then whittled, scraped and sanded down to the diameter desired, usually about 5/16 inch to 11/32 inch in diameter.

When the Cherokees were first contacted by white explorers in 1545, they were using arrows made from cane or reed (Figure 21-2) which Chroniclers described as heavy and stiff and pointed with stone or bone tips. Maurice Thompson, in his book, The Witchery of Archery, describes hunting in Florida and other southern states with cane arrows which were probably the same cane the Cherokees used. Jim Hamm, a bowyer from Texas, makes arrows from Phragmites reed, which may be the same reed that the Cherokees used, although I am not sure. Some tribes other than the Cherokees used cane for arrows. In most instances, the cane was fitted with a wood foreshaft which held the point of the arrow.

When I was a boy, I made most of my arrows from small sprouts of dogwood. Dogwood is very hard, stiff and resistant to breaking. Dogwood should be cut in the winter, the bark peeled and the shafts tied into bundles to help keep them relatively straight while they season for several months (Figure 21-3). The sprouts of other woods such as chokecherry and serviceberry can be gathered and seasoned the same as dogwood. Some of my dogwood arrows shot straight and some didn't and I couldn't figure out why until I learned about arrow spine, which is our next topic.

FIGURE 21-1: Cedar
Arrow Shafts.

FIGURE 21-2: Cane
Arrow Shafts.

FIGURE 21-3: Dogwood Arrow Shafts.

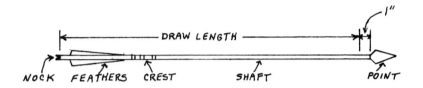

FIGURE 22-1: THE ARROW

FIGURE 22-2: Spine Tester.

CHAPTER 22

ARROW LENGTH AND SPINE

Your understanding of the relationship between arrow length and spine and the draw weight of your bow is a key factor in making arrows that will shoot accurately. Without that understanding, arrow making is mostly a matter of making the arrow and then trying it to see how it will shoot.

The draw length of the arrow (Figure 22-1) is measured from the bottom of the nock, the notch at the back of the arrow that takes the bowstring, to the place on the shaft that comes to the back of the bow handle at your full draw. Or, put another way, the distance from the bowstring to the back of the bow handle at full draw. If you are not sure about your draw length, you may want to refer back to Chapter 9. A quick method for determining the correct draw length for any archer as well as the importance of using as short an arrow as is comfortable are discussed in Chapter 9.

Usually, the arrow is cut so that the back of the broadhead or field point is about one inch beyond the draw length of the shaft (Figure 22-1). Thus, an arrow for a 28 inch draw would be cut so that the length from the bottom of the nock to the back of the point is 29 inches. The extra length allows room for the index finger behind the arrowhead at full draw. With a D bow, the index finger or its knuckle serves as the arrow rest. The handle bow has a shelf arrow rest but many instinctive archers hold the bow so that their index finger is touching the arrow because "feel" is important for instinctive shooting.

The spine of an arrow is a measure of the stiffness of the shaft. The arrow must have the correct spine if it is to shoot accurately from your bow. Primitive bows, whether D bows or handle bows, are not "center shot", that is, if a line were drawn down the center of the bow from tip to tip, the arrow is not on that center line but is to the left of that line for a right handed archer. When the arrow is shot from the bow, it bends around the bow and then quickly recovers its straight line flight to the target. The spine of the arrow determines if the arrow will bend the right amount around the bow. If it is too stiff, the arrow won't bend enough and may hit to the left of the target. If it is not stiff enough, the arrow will bend too much, which will throw it off the target or, if the shaft is very weak, the arrow may even break in the bow.

Arrow spine is usually given in pounds corresponding to the weight bow in which that arrow will shoot correctly. When you buy Port Orford Cedar arrow shafts from a dealer, the shafts will be spined, usually within a five pound range and for a draw length of 28 inches, such as, 45-50 pounds at 28 inches. Buy the shafts whose range covers the draw weight of your bow or the next higher increment, such as, shafts spined 55-60 pounds rather than 50-55 pounds for your 55 pound bow.

Arrow spine is related to the diameter of the shaft; the larger the diameter the stiffer the shaft. Three diameters of shafts are available commercially; 5/16 inch, 11/32 inch and 23/64 inch. The 5/16 shafts are for light bows and spine up to 45 pounds draw weight, the 11/32 shafts will spine from 45 up to 70 pounds and the 23/64 shafts will spine from 70 to well over 100 pounds.

If you wish to cut your own shafts, how can you determine their spine? One way is to purchase a spine tester which works by hanging a weight on the shaft and a guage shows the amount the shaft bends (Figure 22-2). But before I bought a spine tester, I spined many arrows on a device I contrived. I supported the shaft between two notched boards 26 inches apart and hung a weight of two pounds on the center of the shaft. I had a scale marked behind the shaft that I could look at to determine the spine of the shaft. I used commercial cedar shafts of known spine to calibrate the scale. A shaft with a spine of 45 pounds will bend about 1/2 inch while one with a spine of 70 pounds bends about 3/8 inch which is roughly 1/16 inch of bending for each 12 pounds of spine. Of course, this is a rough measure but it is better than no spine testing at all.

Arrow spine is also related to the

length that you draw the shaft. For a constant diameter, the shorter the shaft, the stiffer the spine. I find that, in general, a 5/16 shaft will increase in spine about 7 pounds when you cut the draw length from 28 to 27 inches. An 11/32 shaft will increase about 15 pounds when the draw length is shortened from 28 to 27 inches.

To give you an example of how you can apply this knowledge, at a 28 inch draw, most 5/16 inch diameter cedar shafts will not spine more than 40-45 pounds. But using a 24 inch draw length in a little horse bow I made, I can shoot 5/16 inch diameter cedar shafts in that bow that pulls 65 pounds. The plains Indians used a draw length of 22 or 23 inches which allowed them to use small diameter arrows in very powerful bows. The little arrows are light and shoot very fast but accuracy and penetration are not as good as with a longer bow and heavier arrows.

This whole business of arrow length, diameter, weight and spine seems complicated but it soon will become second nature to you and you will be able to make arrows that suit your needs. Also, whether you make your own bow or shoot with a fiberglass longbow or recurve, it is a great feeling to shoot arrows that you have made yourself.

CHAPTER 23

ARROW STRAIGHTENING

At some point in the process of preparing your arrow shafts, you will need to straighten them. Even with commercial cedar shafts, you will find that most of them are not straight and will require some straightening. If you have cut or split and seasoned your own shafts, you will probably need to straighten them before you size and spine them and then straighten them again after they are sized.

When it comes to arrow shafts, how straight is straight enough? Of course, we would like all our arrows to be perfectly straight but, to be practical, that is something we seldom achieve. If we can get the shafts reasonably straight and fletch the arrows so they spin during flight, they will usually shoot more accurately than we are capable of shooting them.

If the shaft is not too crooked, I straighten it without heating the shaft. I sight down the shaft, while turning it in my fingers, to check it for straightness (Figure 23-1). If I see a crooked place in the wood, I use the fingers and the heel of the thumb of my left hand to bend the shaft in the direction opposite the crook with enough force to straighten the crooked place (Figure 23-2). I continue the process until I have removed all the crooks and the shaft is straight. This straightening is all that is needed with commercial cedar shafts. However, with shafts I have made, I often need to heat the shafts to straighten them. I grease the shafts with bacon drippings and heat the wood over a flame until it is uncomfortable to the touch, which takes only a minute or two. Then I sight down the shaft and work out the crooks with my hands.

After arrows have been straightened, they usually remain straight but I recheck them often to be sure. I usually check the straightness of all the arrows in my quiver before I set out on a day's hunt and, after I have taken a shot at an animal and retrieve my arrow, I check it for straightness. If the arrow has hit a rock or log or if the animal fell on the arrow, the shaft may have cracked and could break as I shot it the next time. But anytime an arrow is subjected to enough stress to crack it, it will be bent and I find the crack when I check the straightness. As I bend the shaft with my hands to straighten it, I will see the crack or the shaft will often break in two. If I discover a crack, I immediately break the shaft in two and put it in my quiver so I won't shoot it by mistake and I can salvage the feathers and point later.

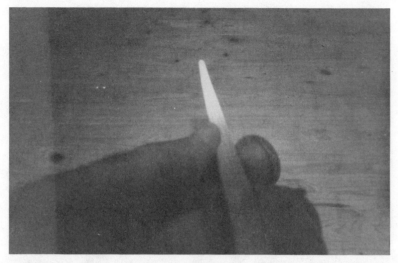

FIGURE 23-1: Sighting Down Arrow Shaft. Shaft is slightly crooked.

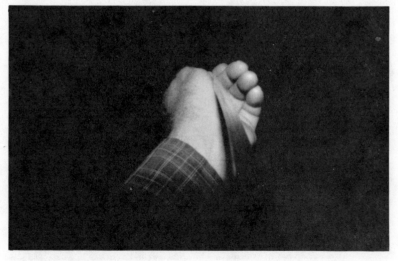

FIGURE 23-2: Bending Shaft to Remove Crooked Place.

FIGURE 23-3: Alex England, Master Bowyer.

CHAPTER 24

ARROW SIZING AND SPINING

In Chapters 9 and 22, we discussed the relationship between the diameter, length and spine of your arrows and the draw weight and length of your bow. If you use commercial cedar shafts, the shafts will come from the supplier to you in the diameter and spine you need to match the weight of your bow. You may need to do a little straightening and sanding of the shafts and then they are ready for cresting and fletching.

If you make your own arrow shafts, you will need to size and spine the shafts. Sizing refers to reducing the diameter of the shafts until they are of the diameter and spine you want. Spine refers to the stiffness of the shaft and was discussed in Chapter 22. The shafts you might make yourself are usually from sprouts of

dogwood or other wood or from split blocks
of black locust or other wood which, in
either case, are larger in diameter than
the finished shafts will be. After the
shafts have properly seasoned, you will
remove wood by whittling, scraping or
sanding to reduce the diameter and spine.
The spine will be reduced a s you reduce
the diameter of the shaft and you stop
whittling when the spine is in the range
you want.

The spine of arrow shafts will vary
greatly from one kind of wood to another
and among shafts made from the same kind
of wood. For example, random commercial
cedar shafts of 11/32 inch diameter and at
a 28 inch draw length will vary in spine
from 30 pounds to over 100 pounds.
Different woods also have different
degrees of stiffness so you will need to
experiment with your wood to find the
diameter that will give you the
approximate spine you want. I will give
you some examples with samples taken from
my stocks of arrows.

All of the following were spined at
a draw length of 28 inches and on
the edge grain of the shaft which
has the maximum spine:
Sample 1: Three arrows made of osage
orange, all with a diameter of 5/16
inch, spined 43 pounds, 34 pounds
and 50 pounds.
Sample 2: Three arrows split from
the same block of black locust wood,
all with a diameter of 5/16 inch,
spined 63 pounds, 57 pounds and 47
pounds.
Sample 3: Two black locust arrows
with diameters of 11/32 and 3/8 inch
spined 66 and 160 pounds
respectively.

Sample 4: Three dogwood arrows as follows: 5/16 inch diameter spined 42 pounds, 11/32 inch spined 73 pounds and 23/64 inch spined 150 pounds.

The examples above clearly illustrate why the arrowmakers of old generally made an arrow and then had to shoot it to see if it would fly right from a particular bow. They used a sizing tool to make all the shafts the same diameter but making arrows of the same diameter still allows for great variation in spine. So, you will want to simultaneously size and spine your arrows with the knowledge that it is more important to match the shafts in spine than in diameter.

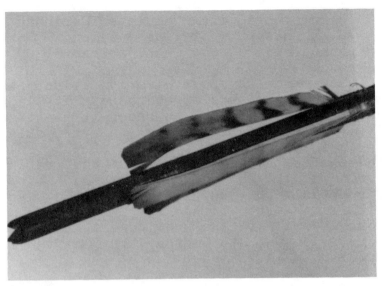

FIGURE 25-1: Traditional Cherokee Nock and Fletching.

FIGURE 25-2: Traditional Cherokee Method of Drawing the Arrow.

CHAPTER 25

ARROW NOCKS AND POINTS

We will assume that you now have a set of arrow shafts that you have purchased or made yourself that are sized and spined for your bow. Your next steps will be to equip the shafts with nocks, cut the shafts to length, and make them ready for points.

If you choose to use commercially made plastic nocks, you need to taper one end of each shaft at an angle of 11 degrees to receive the nock. You can buy a little tapering tool (Figure 25-3) for a few dollars that looks like a pocket pencil sharpener with two holes and cuts tapers for both nocks and points. If you don't have a tapering tool, you can whittle the tapers with a pocket knife. Make sure the tapers are even all around so the nocks are straight when you glue them on. Taper

all the shafts and use glue such as
Elmer's Clear Household Cement, Duco
Cement, or Fletch-Tite to glue the nocks
on the shafts.

If you prefer not to use commercial
plastic nocks on your arrows, you can
whittle, saw or rasp a nock into the wood
of the shaft. The traditional Cherokee
nock (Figure 25-1) is a shallow groove
that is held against the string rather
than sliding over the string. A pinch
type draw is necessary when using this
type nock; the nock is pinched between the
thumb and index finger while the middle
and ring fingers pull the string (Figure
25-2). Some tribes, such as the Sioux,
cut deeper nocks into the wood so the nock
would slide over the string and they used
the three finger, Mediterranean draw used
by modern archers. These deep nocks are
subjected to a lot of stress, especially
from a heavy bow, so the shaft just below
the nock should be reinforced to prevent
the sides of the nock from splitting off.
Most Indians wrapped them with sinew but,
if you don't have sinew, you can
substitute thread wrapped in glue.

Next, measure and cut the shafts to
length. Make sure you allow enough length
for the taper that goes into the point and
an extra inch for your index finger when
you draw. Most tapers for broadheads or
field points are five degrees and require
about 3/4 inch of arrow length but you
should measure to be sure how much your
points require. If you leave 3/4 inch for
the taper and an inch for your finger, you
need to cut your shafts 1-3/4 inches
longer than your draw length. So for a 28
inch draw length, you would cut your
shafts 29-3/4 inches long. Measure from
the bottom of the nock, where the string

goes, mark the correct length, and cut the shaft off.

You may want to taper your shafts and attach the points now or wait until later. When you do, taper the shafts with the tapering tool or your knife. It is vital that this taper be straight because if the broadhead is not on straight your arrow may fly off the mark. Use a hot-melt cement such as Ferr-L-Tite to glue the points on the shafts (Figure 25-4). Melt the tip of the glue stick over a flame (I use a candle) and wipe a little onto the tapered tip of the arrow. Hold the broadhead or field point with pliers over the flame until it is hot enough to melt the glue and then twist the point onto the arrow to spread the glue evenly. Turn the blade of the broadhead to the angle you want it. I line my single-blade broadheads with the slot in the nock so the broadhead will be vertical when I shoot it. When the glue cools and hardens, it will hold the point securely. If you want to remove the point, just heat it and pull it off.

If you prefer to make your own points rather than using commercial points, you can make them from stone or bone, as the pre-Columbian Indians did, or from metal, as the Indians did after they were able to get metal from the white man (Figure 25-5). The making of such arrowheads is a topic worthy of its own book and beyond the scope of our present discussion. There are books available on the subject and I plan to write one myself one day. Such points are fitted into a slot in the end of the arrow shaft and tied to the shaft with sinew or, if metal, made with a socket to fit over the end of the shaft.

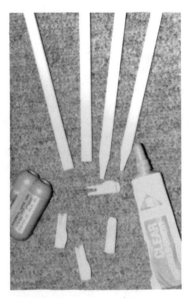

FIGURE 25-3: Attaching Nocks.

FIGURE 25-4: Attaching Points.

FIGURE 25-5: Homemade Arrow Points. Clockwise; 3 flint points, steel broadhead, 2 blunts (cartridges), cornstalk spike, 2 small game points.

CHAPTER 26

ARROW CRESTING AND FINISHING

The "crest" of your arrows refers to the colored markings used to decorate and identify them (Figure 26-1). The "finish" refers to the lacquer, oil or other substance you apply to protect the shaft. You have your choice of putting on the crest and finish before you fletch the arrows (attach the feathers), or waiting until after they are fletched. The advantage of applying the crest and finish before the fletching is that, if you wish, you can dip the shafts rather than using a brush.

Cresting is an ancient tradition. The Indians of old put cresting on their arrows to show ownership, for religious reasons, and for pure decoration. After a battle or a communal hunt, the enemies or game killed could be credited to the warriors or hunters who killed them by the arrows found in the bodies.

Cresting can be simple or elaborate. I use a simple crest; I dip about 10 inches of the shaft in yellow paint before I taper the shaft for a nock. After the paint is dry, I dip the entire shaft in sanding lacquer for a finish. For my big game hunting arrows, I use yellow feathers. Since deer and other mammals I hunt are color blind, the yellow color appears as gray to them but I can see and follow the flight of my arrow when I shoot, see it in the animal to know if I made a hit and also find the arrow more easily if I miss. Some archers make a motor driven apparatus to spin the shaft so they can use small brushes to paint rings around the shaft of different widths and colors, making beautiful crests.

FIGURE 26-1: Five Arrows With Crests.

Howard Hill and Fred Bear made movies
of bowhunting and, to make their arrows
show up well, they used white cresting and
feathers. While watching a Fred Bear
film, I thought the white cresting and
feathers looked neat so I decided to try
white feathers and cresting on an antelope
hunt in New Mexico. I got a big surprise;
those antelope would spot my quiver of
white arrows a mile away and take off for
the next county because white is an alarm
signal to them! Luckily, I found an old
can of blue spray paint in my car and
sprayed my arrows, feathers and all. It
solved the problem and I killed a nice
buck antelope that afternoon. I told Fred
Bear that story later and we had a good
laugh over it. But my point is this:
choose a crest that will help you see your
arrows but which will not spook the game
you seek. For example, if you are turkey
hunting, don't use a crest of bright
colors because turkeys are not color
blind.

If you choose to put the cresting and
finish on your shafts before you fletch
them, you must be sure you use a glue to
attach the feathers that will stick on the
paint you are using. For many years, I
used Duco Cement and glued my feathers on
the bare wood and then crested and
finished my arrows, painting the shaft
between the feathers with a brush because
the Duco would not stick on the paint I
used for cresting and finishing. Now, I
use Anchor brand Flexi-Coat acrylic
exterior latex paint (yellow) for the
cresting, Anchor brand lacquer sanding
sealer over the cresting and the entire
shaft, and then glue the feathers on with
Elmer's Clear Household Cement. Of
course, there are many brands and types of

paints and glues that will work but you must find a combination that works.

I made the apparatus for dipping my arrows (Figure 26-2). I used a piece of aluminum tent pole about one inch in diameter and three feet long that would hold paint and cut the top from a funnel and sealed it to the open top of the aluminum pole. The funnel makes it easy to pour paint into the dipping tube and, as I dip the arrow, the paint overflows from the tube into the funnel so it doesn't spill.

If you prefer to use all natural products in your arrows, you can make paints or dyes from natural pigments for cresting. In the olden days, many Indian tribes used red and black dyes for cresting; the red signified day and black signified night and, together, they gave accuracy to the arrow. If you want to try it, poke berry juice makes a pretty good red and ground charcoal mixed in blood makes a black dye. For a finish on the arrows, rub the shafts with grease from a bear or hog.

FIGURE 26-2: Tools For Dipping Arrow Shafts.

CHAPTER 27

ARROW FLETCHING

The feathers straighten the arrow's flight after it leaves the bow and keeps it in a straight line during its free flight. The feathers are often referred to as the fletching and the process of attaching feathers to an arrow is called by the same name.

There are other materials, such as plastic, which can be used as fletching on an arrow but, for primitive arrows to be used in primitive bows, materials other than feathers do not seem appropriate. There is also a practical reason for using feathers for fletching. There is no other material that works as well as feathers. A D bow requires the shooter to use his knuckle or finger for an arrow rest and a handle bow has a solid shelf that serves as an arrow rest. Arrows with plastic fletching do not shoot well from either type of rest because the stiff plastic causes the arrow to flip. But feathers will flatten out as the arrow passes the arrow rest and then straighten up to guide the arrow in flight.

Usually, the wing feathers of turkeys are the feathers used to fletch arrows. Tail feathers are usually not used because they are not as strong as the wing feathers. A whole feather (Figure 27-1) consists of a stiff "quill" with a flexible "vane" on each side of the quill. The back or trailing vane is wider and stiffer than the leading vane. The trailing vane, attached to a thin strip of the quill, is used for fletching while the leading vane is usually discarded.

Archery shops sell turkey feathers which have been split and the quill ground down ready for gluing to the shaft. You can buy these full length to be cut and shaped the way you want them or you can buy them pre-cut to length and shape (Figure 27-2). The feathers you buy will be designated right or left wing (Figure 27-3). The right wing and left wing feathers are opposite. Many archery shops sell only right wing feathers. Right wing feathers are more readily available because commercial fletchers use left wing feathers. If you buy a fletching jig, make sure you get one for right wing feathers or that you can set for either right or left wing. Don't mix right and left wing feathers on the same arrow because it won't fly right.

Up to about ten years ago, you could buy "gray-barred" feathers from the bronze turkey. Today, all the turkey farmers have switched to the white turkeys so the gray-barred feathers are no longer

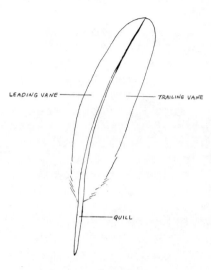

FIGURE 27-1: THE FEATHER

LEADING VANE

TRAILING VANE

QUILL

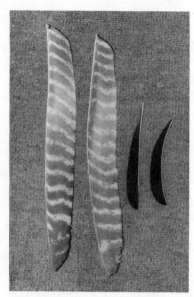

FIGURE 27-2: Full-Length and Die-Cut Feathers.

FIGURE 27-3: Right and Left Wings From "Gray-Bar" Turkey.

FIGURE 27-4: Fletching Jig.

available. It is a shame since the gray-barred feathers were stronger than the white turkey feathers and also I liked the way they looked; sort of a natural camouflage. You can buy the white turkey feathers dyed various colors and they are even coloring an imitation gray-bar now, but it just isn't the same as the real thing. I manage to get a few wild turkey wings each year from birds I kill or as gifts from fellow hunters and I use the gray-barred feathers for special arrows.

If you will be fletching quite a few arrows each year, it would be wise for you to buy a fletching jig (Figure 27-4). The jig holds the arrow shaft and the feather in a clamp so that each feather is glued on at the same angle and it simplifies the job of fletching. I have three jigs that each put on one feather at a time or you can get a jig that will put on three feathers at once. But you don't have to have a fletching jig; you can do as good a job with a few straight pins. It just takes longer.

If you have purchased feathers that have the quills split and ground and are die cut to shape, you need only glue the feathers to the shaft. The feathers are usually attached to the shaft at an angle which causes the arrow to spin and stabilize in flight. The angle is set to expose the underside of the feather to the air so it is angled one way for right wing feathers and the opposite for left wing feathers (Figure 27-5). Looking at the feather from the nock end of the arrow, a right wing feather, from back to front, is angled to the right while a left wing feather, from back to front, is angled to the left.

If you have feathers that have the

quills split and ground but are left full length, you will need to cut them to length, glue them to the arrow shaft and then trim them to the shape you want. The length you cut the feathers will depend on your intended use of the arrows. For hunting arrows with broadheads, you should use feathers five inches long; for target arrows from a light bow, three or four inches long; and for flight arrows to be shot for distance, perhaps one inch long. Usually you will glue the feathers to the shaft and then trim the feathers to the height and shape you want.

If you have whole turkey wing feathers, you will need to split the quill and grind the quill down until it is thin and flat. It helps to have a clamp, such as the clamp from a fletching jig, to hold the feather while you grind it against a grinder or use your knife and a file.

There is a way that is easier, if you can learn to do it, which I call "stripping" the feather. Starting at the tip of the feather, carefully pull the trailing vane away from the quill with your fingers (Figure 27-6). You want to pull a thin "skin" off the quill rather than splitting the quill. When you have the thin skin, with the vane attached, separating from the quill, simply peel it off toward the base of the quill. Cut the fletch to length and it is ready to glue to the shaft.

Now you are ready to fasten the feathers onto the shaft. If you have a fletching jig, set the angles for your clamps for right or left wing feathers and for the amount of spin you want on your arrows. Put the arrow shaft in the jig and put feathers in the clamps. Run a thin bead of glue on the quill of the feather and then clamp the feather against the arrow shaft until the glue sets.

If you don't have a fletching jig, you can use pins to hold the feathers in place until the glue sets (Figure 27-7). If the quills are stiff, you can lay the feathers on a wet towel to soften them so they are easier to handle. I like to stick a pin in the quill at the front and back of the feather before I try to put it on the arrow shaft. This first feather will be the "cock feather" which is perpendicular to the slot in the nock and will stick out perpendicular from the bow when the arrow is on the string. Some archers like this cock feather to be a different color so they can quickly identify it and see how to nock the arrow.

I pin the back of the cock feather to the shaft an inch below the bottom of the nock slot by sticking the pin into the wood, and then angle the feather the way I want it and pin the front of the feather to the wood. I space and pin the other two feathers in place. Finally, I run a thin bead of glue along the quill and arrow shaft by each feather. When the glue has set, I remove the pins.

Traditional Cherokee arrows have the feathers attached to the arrow shaft by tying with sinew rather than being glued (Figure 27-8). The feather is stripped or the quill split and ground down flat. The feather is cut to length with a strip of quill about one half inch long extending past the vane of the feather at the front and back.

The back extensions of the quills are first wrapped to the shaft with wet sinew and then the feathers are folded forward on the shaft so the wrapping will be under the back of the finished fletching. The

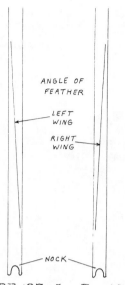

FIGURE 27-5: Feather Angle.

FIGURE 27-6: Stripped Feather.

FIGURE 27-7: Feather Ready For Gluing.

FIGURE 27-8: Sinew Tied Feathers.

137

feathers are angled to give spin to the arrow and the front extensions of the quills are wrapped onto the shaft with wet sinew. The wet sinew makes its own glue so, when it is dry, the arrow is ready to shoot. Usually, the middle part of the quill, between the sinew wraps, is not attached to the shaft.

You can trim the feathers to shape by several methods. You can buy a sharp metal "chopper" of the correct shape and cut the feathers by hitting the chopper with a block. I used to have a feather burner made from a model train transformer and a piece of nichrome wire I bent to the shape I wanted. The wire got red hot and burned the feathers off to the correct height and shape as I turned the arrow against the wire. Or, you can just use scissors to trim the feathers. You will probably do a lot of experimenting with different shaped feather trims until you find one you like best.

After the feathers are attached to the shaft and trimmed, I trim the front tip of the quill with a sharp knife and put a drop of glue on it to make a smooth surface. A sharp tip on the front of the quill may cut your finger when you shoot the arrow or strip the feather off the shaft if you have to pull the arrow through a target.

CHAPTER 28

DOUBLE LOOP BOWSTRINGS

You may want to make your own
bowstrings for several reasons; you will
have the satisfaction of having made all
the equipment that you use, you can make a
better string than you can buy, and you
may have trouble buying a string to fit
your bow.

I can make the traditional Cherokee
bowstrings of rawhide and I will tell you
how to do it in the next chapter but I
primarily use double loop dacron strings
for my shooting and hunting. I make these
strings and I do not feel they are a
serious violation of the spirit of
primitive archery which I follow. I
prefer the dacron strings to the rawhide
strings for several reasons. Foremost is
the fact that the rawhide strings are
about 1/8 inch in diameter which is too

large for a deep notch type nock. Therefore a shallow nock must be used and that necessitates a pinch-type draw. A pinch-type draw is all right for light bows up to 50 pounds draw weight but I have trouble drawing my 70 and 80 pound hunting bows with a pinch draw because it hurts my hand. With a dacron string, I can use a deep notch nock and a three finger draw.

You can buy a spool of Dacron B string material, a spool of serving thread, and some bowstring wax and have enough material to make many strings (Figure 28-1). If you will be making several strings, you may want to invest in or build a string jig although you can do the same job with a few large nails. I will illustrate how to make a string using a string jig and you can easily apply the information to making a string with nails. A little string serving tool is also handy; I made mine from a strip of thin metal, a long bolt with a wing nut and a couple of washers. With this equipment, you are ready to make strings anywhere.

I always take a spool of dacron and some nails with me on hunting trips. I have made many emergency strings in camp that saved the hunt for me or hunting companions after accidently cutting or breaking bowstrings. On one hunting trip in the Colorado Rockies, I made a companion four strings in one day to replace strings broken by his compound bow that wasn't tuned right or something. I kept making them heavier until the last one held.

Before you make a string, you need to determine how long to make it to fit your bow. Of course, if you have a string that is the correct length you merely measure it and make another the same length. But if you have just made a new bow or if your old string broke, you need a way to determine the length of string you need. I have measured many bows and strings and calculated a ratio that I use to determine the length of the double loop string I need for any length longbow. I measure the length of the bow between the string nocks and multiply that measurement by .954. The product is a close approximation of the length of the string I need. I usually round the product up to the next half inch. For example, if the calculated length was 62.15 inches, I would round the figure to 62-1/2 inches. If the string is a little too long, I can twist it and make it a little shorter. If it is too short, there is nothing to do but make another string.

After you have determined the length string you need, set your string jig to that length. If you are using nails, drive two 16 penny nails that distance apart in a plank, log or other rigid piece of wood. My string jig has metal pins in the tops of the arms so, when I use the term pin, I am talking about the pins on the string jig. Hold or tie the end of the dacron string at one pin (or nail), then unwind string off the spool and take it down and around the other pin (or nail), then back to the first pin, continuing the loops of string until you have the number of strands recommended for your bow weight (Figure 28-2). Wrap the string just under the head at the top of the pins (or nails) and be careful not to cross the string between pins so, when you finish, you have half the strands on one side and half on the other with the pins dividing the two halves. Cut the string

FIGURE 28-1: String
Material.

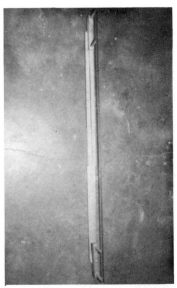

FIGURE 28-2: Wrap
On Dacron String.

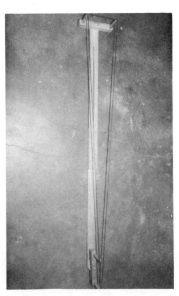

FIGURE 28-3: Spread
the String.

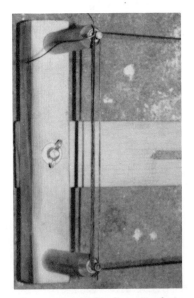

FIGURE 28-4: Rein-
force the Loop.

FIGURE 28-5: Serve
the Loop.

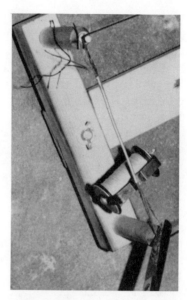

FIGURE 28-6: Cut Re-
inforcment Strings.

FIGURE 28-7: Center
the Served Section.

FIGURE 28-8: Close
the Loop.

loose from the spool, leaving some extra for tying a knot, and then tie the two ends of the dacron string together in a square knot. Position the knot so it will be wrapped under the serving thread in one of the string loops when the string is finished.

Now you will form the loops at each end of the string. If you are using a string jig, turn the arm at one end of the jig so the string goes around two pins instead of one. If you are using nails, slip the string off of the nail at one end and drive two "new" nails which will spread the end of the string a distance of six or eight inches and still hold it tight (Figure 28-3). As a result, the string will look like a long triangle, looping around the two pins to form the base of the triangle and around the single pin at the other end to form the peak of the triangle.

I like to reinforce my loops; otherwise the loops will contain only half the number of strands that the main string contains. So on a 12 strand string, I put six extra, short strands in the loop so it will also be 12 strands thick (Figure 28-4). I wrap dacron string from the spool around the two pins until I have my six extra strands, cut the string loose from the spool and tie a knot in the ends of the string. When I have finished the loop, this string will reinforce the loop.

After you have put in you reinforcement string, rub string wax on the string and reinforcement string. Now you are ready to wrap serving thread around the string and reinforcement string between the two pins to form a loop on the end of your string. You will wrap serving thread on the string for a distance of two

to four inches, depending on the size loop
you want. Unless the tips of your bow
limbs are very narrow or wide, about three
inches will make a suitable loop. Measure
where you need to begin the serving to
center it between the two pins. Wrap over
the end of the serving thread to begin the
serving (Figure 28-5).

When you have wrapped the length for
your loop, hold the serving thread tight,
take scissors and cut through the
reinforcement strings at each end between
the serving and the pin, being careful not
to cut your main strings (Figure 28-6).
Now turn the arm of the string jig so the
string loops around only one pin or, if
you are using nails, slip the string off
the two nails and slip it back over the
original nail. If the wrapped portion is
not centered on the pin (or nail), slip
the string around the pin until it is
centered on the pin (Figure 28-7).

Now, to close the loop, continue to
wrap the serving around both halves of the
string and continue the serving past the
loose ends of the reinforcement strands
for an inch or more (Figure 28-8). Then
tie off the serving and put a drop of glue
on the end to help hold it.

Repeat the process on the other end to
form the other loop.

After you have both loops complete,
try the string on your bow to make sure it
is the right length. For a handle bow six
feet long, the correct "fistmele" or
distance from the belly of the handle to
the string is about 6-1/2 inches and for a
six foot D bow the fistmele should be
about 7-1/2 inches (Figure 28-9). The
fistmele will be less for shorter bows.
If the fistmele is a little too low,
unstring the bow and twist the string

until it is right.

Finally, wrap serving onto the center of the string to protect it from abrasion from your shooting glove and your arm guard as you shoot your bow (Figure 28-10). With your bow strung, rub the entire string with string wax and then rub the string rapidly with a piece of newspaper folded around it. The friction will heat the wax and drive it into the string. Occasionally, rewax your string. If you should break a strand or two of your bowstring, you should replace the bowstring because, if the bowstring breaks during a shot, your bow can be damaged. So, it is a good idea to always carry a spare bowstring.

FIGURE 28-9: Measure Fistmele.

FIGURE 28-10: Serve Center of String.

CHAPTER 29

RAWHIDE BOWSTRINGS

Now, I will tell you how to make a traditional Cherokee rawhide bowstring. I have read that Cherokees made bowstrings from sinew but I have never seen one being used by Cherokees. I suspect those writers saw a bowstring made of rawhide and mistook it for sinew. Of course, a bowstring can be made from sinew and some tribes used sinew bowstrings so it is possible that, long ago, Cherokees used sinew strings. But if they did, I can't understand why the practice would not have been handed down to us today as was the practice of making rawhide strings.

The traditional rawhide bowstrings are usually made from the hide of a fox squirrel or groundhog. There is a lot of difference in the toughness of the hides of different animals and the rawhide from an old fox squirrel or groundhog is stronger and will last longer than any other I have tried.

The hide can be stretched and the hair scraped off with a scraper but I prefer a method my father taught me; I use wood ashes which I save from my fireplace and cookstove. After fleshing the hide, I put the hide in a shallow wooden trough, hair side up, and put several inches of ashes over it. I pour water on the ashes until I have a paste. The water extracts a chemical (potassium hydroxide), which is like lye, from the ashes which causes the hair to loosen from the hide. As a side note, with the water from the ashes mixed with animal fat you can make soft soap.

It may take anywhere from one day to a week for the hair to slip, depending on the strength of the ashes, the condition of the hide and the temperature of the air. I keep checking the hide until I can slip the hair off with my fingers, then I take it out, stretch it over a smooth log and pull or scrape off the hair. When I have all the hair off, I wash the hide with soap in the river and stretch it with nails on my barn wall until I am ready to use it.

When you are ready to make a bowstring, soften the rawhide in water and trim the hide with scissors to make it approximately round. Then, with scissors, cut a thin strip around the edge of the hide in a continuous circle toward the center (Figure 29-1). If you cut it thin, even a squirrel hide will make a strand many feet long. Cut the strands off about 12 to 14 feet long; the 12 foot length for a bow five to five and a half feet long and the 14 foot length if your bow is six feet long. I cut two strands for a light bow and three for a heavy bow. They will be doubled so the light bowstring contains four of the rawhide strands and the heavy bowstring contains six.

Next, form the loop in the bowstring. For our discussion, let's say you are making a bowstring with four rawhide strands for a bow about five feet long. First, drive a nail in a board wall or a tree seven or eight feet above the ground. Wet each rawhide strand and double it in the middle over the nail so that each 12 foot strand makes two six foot strands hanging from the nail or a total of four strands hanging down. Twist the four strands together for a length of about four inches below the nail (Figure 29-2).

We want to make a loop, not a slip knot in the end of the string. If you put the ends of all four strands through the little loop that is over the nail, you would make a slip knot that would tighten when you put it on the nock of your bow. To make a loop that doesn't slip, hold all four strands together at the end of the twisted length and, with your other hand, reach down and get the loose ends of two of the strands, bring them up and slip them through the loop that is over the nail (Figure 29-3). Pull them through until the end of the twisted section pulls up to the loop. In other words, two strands go through the loop and the other two strands do not. This forms the loop in the end of the string that doesn't slip. Remove the loop from the nail and hang the larger loop (the one you just made) on the nail (Figure 29-4).

Now knot the ends of the four hanging strands together and tie them to the bail of a bucket and put some rocks in the bucket for weight (Figure 29-5). Spin the

bucket to twist the strands together over
the whole length of the bowstring. Then
leave the bucket hanging on the bowstring
until the rawhide is dry. The bucket
hanging against the wall will prevent the
bowstring form untwisting and the weight
will stretch the rawhide. When the
rawhide is dry, the string will stay
twisted.

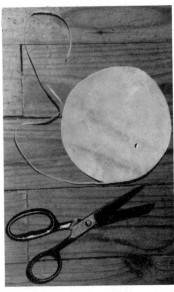

FIGURE 29-1: Cut
the Rawhide.

FIGURE 29-2: First
Step in Forming
Loop.

FIGURE 29-3: Half
the Strands Through
Small Loop.

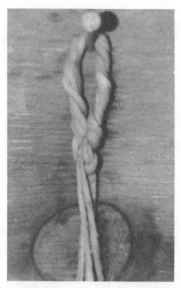

FIGURE 29-4: The
Finished Loop.

FIGURE 29-5: Weight
On String.

FIGURE 29-6: String
On Bow.

To put the rawhide string on your bow, slip the loop over the upper end of the bow and down the bow limb a few inches. Then tie the string on the nock of the lower limb, wrapping and making several half hitches so it will hold (Figure 29-6). Then, string the bow and check the "fistmele" height. The fistmele is the distance from the string to the back of the handle of the bow; normally a distance of about 6-1/2 inches for a handle bow and about 7-1/2 inches for a D bow. Many traditional archers determine the fistmele height by standing their fist and extended thumb, hitchhiker style, on the back of the bow handle. The approximate fistmele height is at or a little above the tip of the thumb. You may have to unstring the bow, untie the knots on the lower nock and adjust the length of the string to get the correct fistmele height.

If the nocks on your bow are shallow, they may not hold the rawhide string and you may have to cut the nocks deeper. Traditional Cherokee bows made for rawhide bowstrings have deep, V shaped nocks with the edges left sharp to help keep the tied end from slipping. The sharp edges would quickly wear a dacron string in two but the rawhide is very tough.

A rawhide string is very durable and will take many years of shooting. If you wish, you can rub wax on your rawhide string to give it some protection from moisture but, in a downpour, it will still get wet and stretch a little.

CHAPTER 30

SHOOTING THE CHEROKEE BOW

Shooting a Cherokee bow without sights is quite different from shooting a compound bow with sights. If you have good shooting form with the compound, it will help you in learning to shoot the Cherokee bow. But there are also new things to learn and you may discover, as many have, that shooting a Cherokee bow by methods that the Cherokees have used for thousands of years will open up a new and exciting kind of archery for you.

INSTINCTIVE SHOOTING

The traditional Cherokee method of "aiming" a bow and arrow is "instinctive", without any sighting devices on the bow. I can best describe the process by comparing it to pitching a baseball or shooting a basketball in which you send the ball toward the target by "feel". Trying to "aim" your shot is actually detrimental to your accuracy. To shoot a bow instinctively, you look at the spot you want to hit, without trying to align anything on the bow or arrow with the target, allow your instincts to aim your shot and release the arrow when it "feels" right.

The key to instinctive shooting is to concentrate on the spot you want to hit. The bullseye of a target helps you concentrate but, if your target has no bullseye, such as a deer or other animal, you must visualize a spot on the animal and aim at that spot. Otherwise, you will tend to shoot at the whole animal and probably miss. When I shoot at a deer, I shoot at the spot where the back edge of the fore leg intersects the belly line. I tend to shoot high when shooting at deer so shooting at that spot usually puts my arrow through the heart or lungs. It also helps, when shooting at any target, to visualize a small spot rather than a large spot. If you visualize a spot the size of a basketball, you will hit close to it but, if you visualize a spot the size of an aspirin, you will hit close to it and make a better shot.

Most archers in today's world of high technology place little importance on their instincts. But in truth, no electronic or mechanical equipment can compare with the human body in its ability to evaluate its surroundings and make quick and appropriate responses. To me, there is as much difference between an expert instinctive shooter and an expert sight shooter as there is between a good athlete and a robot. That is not meant as a criticism of robots, they do what they were meant to do with efficiency and accuracy, but they do not generate much excitement and they are severely limited in what they can do.

In most hunting situations, the hunter shooting by instinct has a considerable advantage over the sight shooter in being able to quickly react to the situation, whether it be a running rabbit, a flushed cock pheasant or a running whitetailed buck. Generally, the sight shooter does not even consider shooting at such targets while, to the instinctive shooter, such shots are the joy of bowhunting.

STANDING

The term "standing" will not only refer to how you place your feet but to the whole attitude of your body while you are shooting. If you observe a sight shooter, his or her overall body attitude could be described as static during shooting since most of the time involved in the shot is in holding and aiming. By contrast, an instinctive shooter's overall body attitude could be described as fluid since the shooting process appears to be one smooth, continuous motion from the beginning of the draw to the release of the arrow.

Typically, the instinctive shooter's feet are comfortably apart and lined with the target, the legs are not locked at the knees, and the body may be bent forward slightly at the hips. Among traditional Indian archers, the bow arm is not extended toward the target before the shot but is held by the left side or in front of the body or held above the head. At the shot, the bow arm swings into alignment with the target while still slightly bent at the elbow, the bow is canted at an angle, and the shooter's head is at an angle similar to the canted bow so that his eye is above the arrow.

DRAWING, HOLDING and RELEASING

We will discuss drawing, holding and

releasing together because, in instinctive shooting, the three acts occur in one continuous, fluid movement.

Lyman Vann, a Cherokee, was my friend and hunting companion and the best natural instinctive archer I ever knew. When preparing to shoot at a stationary target, Lyman would stand with his bow at his left side and look at the target. As he began his shot, he would quickly swing his bow in an arc upward and then toward the target while simultaneously drawing his bow by a push with his bow arm and a pull with his right arm. When the arrow reached full draw he released instantly and then "followed through" by holding his position for a second or two. His movements in shooting might be described as fluid grace responding to keen instincts.

You can draw slowly or quickly but, whichever you choose, do it consistently. I practice drawing quickly because, while hunting, I often need to take a quick shot.

You should also establish an "anchor point", a spot to which you draw each time. I draw and put the middle finger of my right hand at the corner of my mouth. An anchor point assures that you will get a full draw without your having to look at the tip of your arrow, which is a serious error for an instinctive shooter. Most instinctive archers anchor somewhere on the side of their face between their chin and their cheekbone while most sight shooters anchor below their chin.

Holding refers to the pause between drawing your arrow and releasing. For most instinctive shooters, the pause is brief. Roger Ascham described holding for English archers in 1545. He wrote, "Holdynge must not be longe, for it bothe putteth a bowe in jeopardy, and also marreth a mans shoot, it must be so lytle (that) it may be perceyved better in a mans mynde when it is done, than seene with a mans eyes when it is in doying." Since the instinctive shooter does not have to line up any sights on the target, there is no reason for holding for an extended time. In fact, when an instinctive shooter holds too long, it is a sign that he doesn't trust his instincts and is attempting to consciously "aim" which usually results in a poor shot.

Release and follow through are two vital parts of good shooting. The fingers must release the string smoothly which is much easier with a heavy bow than with a light bow. During the release, the string must not hit anything such as your clothing.

The follow through consists of maintaining the alignment of all parts of your body with the target after the arrow is released. The Cherokee bow has no stabilizers to prevent twisting in your hand or other movements. The best way to minimize bow movement in the hand after the release is to shoot with a loose grip on the bow. You must also keep your right hand close to your face after you release and hold your bow arm in its position until the arrow strikes the target. A common fault is dropping the bow arm and raising the head to better see where your shot is going. Keep your arm up and your head down until the arrow is in the target, then go and see where you hit.

EMOTIONS

The champion archer or the consistently successful hunter often is no better shot than other archers or hunters but he or she has learned to control his or her emotions. The effect of emotion is greater on an instinctive shooter than on a sight shooter. A faint heart causes more missed shots than any other thing; to always shoot well you must shoot with bold courage. All emotions, but especially anger, will cloud your mind and your instincts and harm your shooting.

PRACTICING FOR HUNTING

Shooting well instinctively requires more practice than shooting well with sights. The bowhunter who shoots instinctively also needs to practice shooting at animal targets under hunting conditions. Animal targets are better than bullseye targets because, with animal targets, the hunter learns to pick an imaginary spot on the animal to place his shot. He should practice also at moving targets such as balloons blown across a lawn by the wind, an old tire rolled down a hill, or a frisbee or cardboard disc thrown in the air. Such targets are fun to shoot and teach skills that a hunter needs.

I also practice rapidly shooting several arrows. Holding two arrows on the back of the bow with my bow hand and with another arrow on the string, I can shoot the three arrows with accuracy in less than ten seconds.

The practice at shooting rapidly at moving targets prepares me for hunting. To give some examples, I often get more than one shot at a deer, if my first shot misses. I shoot at, and often hit, moving game such as running squirrels and rabbits and flying game birds. Of the 32 squirrels I killed with my bow in 1988, about half were taken with running shots. These are the shots that make memories to talk about around the campfires of many years.

BIBLIOGRAPHY

Ascham, R. Toxophilus. London, 1545.

Hamilton, T.M. Native American Bows. Columbia: Missouri Archaeological Society, 1982.

Hill, H. Hunting The Hard Way. Harpersville, AL: Jerry Hill, 1976.

Laubin, R.& G. American Indian Archery. Norman: University of Oklahoma Press, 1980.

Thompson, J.M. The Witchery Of Archery. First printing, 1877. Reprinted at Minot, ND: Kim Fundingsland Productions, 1986.